ACKNOWLEDGEMENTS

To three remarkable women who shaped my life and financial journey in ways I'll always treasure:

To my mother, Helen, who taught me the value of managing money with grace and discipline.

You showed me how to stretch a dollar, run a home, and feed a large family, all on a shoestring budget, while making it look effortless. Your lessons on resourcefulness and financial savvy continue to guide me every day.

To my nan, Norma, whose love, nurturing spirit, and wisdom provided not only comfort but also invaluable lessons in how real estate can generate cash flow. Your cleverness and resilience, especially as a widow, inspired me to think creatively, and take charge of my financial future.

Your teachings on independence and strategic thinking remain as relevant as ever.

To my sister, Michelle, who was always my biggest cheerleader. You taught me the importance of balance in life, reminding me that success is sweeter when it's filled with fun, laughter, and the support of those we love. Your example of joy and balance continues to be my compass.

Though all three of you have passed, your lessons live on in my heart and actions. The wisdom you shared remains as valuable and true today as it ever was. Thank you for your love, guidance, and strength.

MONEY POWER

MASTER MONEY HABITS TO SECURE YOUR FINANCIAL FUTURE

A STEP-BY-STEP GUIDE TO
ELIMINATE DEBT, BUILD WEALTH &
CREATE A LIFE OF FINANCIAL FREEDOM

JANENE O'CONNOR

Copyright © 2025 by Janene O' Connor
All rights reserved.

No part of this publication may be reproduced, distributed, or transmitted in any form or by any means, including photocopying, recording, or other electronic or mechanical methods, without the prior written permission of the author, except in the case of brief quotations embodied in critical reviews and certain other noncommercial uses permitted by copyright law.

For permission requests, contact:
janeneoconnor.com

Disclaimer

The information provided in this book is for educational and inspirational purposes only. It is based on personal experience and general strategies used and should not be considered financial, legal, or taxation advice. I am not a licensed financial planner, adviser, or accountant. Before making any financial decisions or investments, you should seek independent professional advice tailored to your individual circumstances. Every effort has been made to ensure the information is accurate at the time of writing, but readers are encouraged to verify facts and figures and take responsibility for their own financial due diligence.

TABLE OF CONTENTS

Acknowledgements 3
My Story 9
Introduction: Money Habits 15

PART A: WHERE ARE YOU AT NOW? 23
    CHAPTER 1: Awareness Of Your Money Mindset 25
    Section 1: Identifying Your Current Money Beliefs 26
    Section 2: The Impact of Mindset 33
    Section 3: Shifting to a Growth-Oriented Money Mindset ... 36
    Week 1: Small Steps to the Future Abundant You 43

    CHAPTER 2: Balance 45
    Section 1: The Power of Intentional Living 46
    Section 2: The Psychology of Money 47
    Week 2: Small Steps to the Future Abundant You 52

PART B: WHERE 'EXACTLY' DOES YOUR MONEY GO? ... 53
    Chapter 3: Understanding is Power 55
    Section 1: Why Knowing Your Numbers Matters 56
    Section 2: Financial Tracking 61
    Week 3: Small Steps to the Future Abundant You 65

    Chapter 4: Notice - When On or Off Budget 67
    Section 1: Why Budgets Give You Freedom 69
    Section 2: Building Your First and Only Budget 71
    Week 4: Small Steps to the Future Abundant You 81

Chapter 5: Disaster! 83
    Section 1: The Role of an Emergency Fund 84
    Section 2: Creating Your Safety Net 87
    Section 3: Maintaining Your Fund 89
    Section 4: Insurance for Unexpected Events 91
    Week 5: Small Steps to the Future Abundant You 93

Chapter 6: Allocate 95
    Section 1: Why Automation Works 96
    Section 2: Setting Up Automation 100
    Section 3: Maintaining Momentum: Adjusting Automation 104
    Week 6: Small Steps to the Future Abundant You 106

PART C: WHERE DO YOU WANT TO BE? 107
    Chapter 7: Navigate Debt as a Tool 109
    Rule 1: Be Responsible with Credit 110
    Rule 2: Optimize Debt-Repayment Strategies 115
    Rule 3: Borrow Wisely 125
    Week 7: Small Steps to the Future Abundant You 128

    Chapter 8: Compound Interest 129
    Section 1: The Power of Compound Interest 130
    Section 2: Investment Options Explained 134
    Section 3: Creating a Habit of Investing 141
    Week 8: Small Steps to the Future Abundant You 144

    Chapter 9: Evaluate Financial Goals 145
    Section 1: Align Goals with Values 146
    Section 2: SMARTIE Financial Goals 149
    Section 3: Tracking and Adjusting Goals 151
    Week 9: The Future Abundant You 153

Chapter 10: Financial Freedom in Retirement 155
Section 1: Assessing Your Current Financial Position 158
Section 2: Determining Your Retirement Needs 161
Section 3: The Retirement Gap 164
Section 4: Action Steps 166
Section 5: Creating your personalized retirement plan 168

Conclusion: Money Habits for Life 171

MY STORY

I was born in Dubbo, NSW, on a modest farm where the smell of fresh cow manure mixed with the distant sound of my mother Helen's weary voice. She was a formidable woman who suffered the burden of an abusive husband, my step father Brian. He was an alcoholic whose rage often erupted in violence.

Due to having no money of her own, my mother was very much stuck. Brian was the sole breadwinner, so she couldn't afford to toss him out or escape, even if she wanted to. And so, our home felt like a battlefield where we walked in fear that one wrong move would set him off.

MY STORY

Watching my mother stretch every dollar was both awe-inspiring and heartbreaking. She grew her own fruits and vegetables, and raised chickens and cows to keep us fed. Despite her resourcefulness, it was clear that money was scarce, and it had the power to trap you.

In my young mind, money became synonymous with limitations. My stepfather's cutting words echoed in my head with encouraging sentiments like, "You'll never amount to much," and "You're useless." I recall one afternoon coming home from school, bursting with excitement after scoring ninety-eight percent on a math test. Instead of congratulating me, Brian condescendingly said, "Where's the other two percent?" His belittling remarks were a heavy shroud, stifling any sense of pride I might have felt. It didn't matter how hard I worked or how well I performed. I always felt that I was never enough.

My mother, though burdened, was resilient. She often told me, "Study hard, and secure a good job" and reminded me it was the only way to make it in this world. Her beliefs became my guiding principles, reinforcing the notion that hard work was the only path to success. I took her advice to heart and secured a job at Westpac Bank, where I devoted myself to my career, working long hours for minimal wage. In addition, I attended seminars and devoured books on personal development, real estate, and investing, driven by an almost desperate desire to escape the constraints of my upbringing.

But as I worked tirelessly to save for my first investment property, life in Sydney proved to be a harsh reality. The high living expenses made it nearly impossible to scrape together a deposit on my own. I felt frustration mounting, as a voice in my head whispering, "Why do some people have all the money?" It seemed so unfair. I wanted to be free, yet I felt shackled by my circumstances and impatient for success.

My money habits helped me balance my finances without feeling overwhelmed. By sticking to this structure, I was able to demonstrate strong money management skills, which played a crucial role in securing a joint venture partner. At twenty-three, I took a leap of faith and purchased my first home through that joint venture. Less than two years later, we sold it, and I used the profits to buy my very own property. The realization that what I earned had eclipsed four years of my then-annual salary ignited a fire within me and sparked an insatiable hunger to build a real estate portfolio.

MY STORY

I learned that true wealth came from owning assets, not merely exchanging my time for money. I acquired the fundamentals from the Kiyosaki book *Rich Dad Poor Dad*. By thirty-two, I was poised to retire. I thought I'd finally broken free from the cycle of fear and limitation that had defined my early years.

Two years later, I married Neil, a local real estate agent who had a refreshingly laid-back attitude towards life and money. Unlike my stepfather, Neil was a loving man who was grounded, valuing experiences and connection over material wealth. We dove into the business of running multiple real estate offices together, fueled by shared dreams and aspirations, all funded by my money. Life was unfolding perfectly for us. Then on Saturday, July 25, 2005, mere hours after all three of us were singing and dancing to our son Josh's favorite song, the Wiggles *Big Red Car,* Neil died in a car accident, and in an instant, I became a widow at age thirty-seven, left to raise our two-year-old son on my own. The fear that washed over me was suffocating. How could I possibly manage all aspects of our real estate business and care for my son at the same time? I was consumed by overwhelming doubt, confronted with the realization that I was alone.

In my grief, I chose to prioritize my son and closed the business down. Once again, money became a pressing issue, lurking in the shadows of every sleepless night. The burden of debt loomed over me, a relentless reminder of my new reality.

Six months later, still grieving, feeling lost and desperate for connection, I met Danny, a charming developer whose charisma seemed to promise the security I craved. He and his wife presented themselves as saviors; able to help me create the financial stability I'd long sought. I finally felt hopeful, even as caution whispered in my ear. But soon, I would learn that Danny was not what he appeared.

He turned out to be a fraud, leaving me with a staggering $300,000 in debt after I was forced to sell all of my assets to settle the mess he'd created. The legal battles that ensued drained me emotionally and financially. I felt like I was trapped in a nightmare, constantly questioning how I would meet my bills each month, let alone provide for my son. Have you ever felt like no matter what you do, there just isn't enough to go around? That was my daily reality.

MY STORY

Eight years later, I found Barry; a kind and supportive man who became my partner in every sense of the word. When we married, I was determined to take charge of our financial future. I jokingly said to him, "You earn the money, and I'll spend it." But this was a lighthearted comment that masked a deeper fear of losing control over my finances. Together, we borrowed to invest in real estate, and I took charge of researching, conducting due diligence, purchasing, and managing our projects.

The road was anything but smooth. We faced many challenges along the way, including builders going bankrupt and projects exceeding budgets due to unexpected variations in contracts. Balancing cash flow and managing large sums of money became daily hurdles that I had to confront head-on. Each challenge reignited my fears of financial instability, repeating past mistakes. and being a failure. Yet, with every success, my confidence grew. The first project proved fruitful, a turning point that slowly chipped away at my anxiety and self-doubt.

Fast forward seven and a half years, and we reached a pivotal moment when we could finally retire. I began coaching, focusing on how money beliefs impact daily decisions around managing finances, building assets, and investing. I wanted to help others understand that their fears and beliefs about money could either limit or empower them.

Today, Barry and I enjoy the freedom of being self-funded retirees, independent of government support. We relish our time with family and friends, exploring and doing what we love. I still check in on our finances each week to make sure that our money is working for us, a tool for the life we've built together.

Throughout this journey of self-discovery, I learned to confront my fears head-on. The feelings of inadequacy instilled by my stepfather began to lose its grip on me. I no longer defined my worth by the words of others and realized that money was merely an instrument that could help create the life I desired. I transformed from a girl who felt limited by her upbringing to a woman who uses money as a means of creating a life of abundance and joy.

In helping others navigate their finances, I find empowerment in sharing my story. I encourage you to confront your fears, challenge your beliefs, and embrace the possibility of financial independence. My life is no longer dictated by the limitations of my past. Instead, it's fueled by the hope and determination of building a brighter future for myself and my family. The cycle of fear has been broken, and I'm now the author of my own narrative, rewriting the story of my life with every step I take towards financial freedom.

INTRODUCTION

Money Habits

The surprising truth is that wealth isn't just about how much you earn but what you do with what you earn. Sustainable wealth is built from the small, intentional choices you make every day. Let's explore how changing your money habits can change your financial life, no matter your income.

INTRODUCTION

PURPOSE

WHY FINANCIAL HABITS MATTER MORE THAN INCOME

If you've ever thought, *I'd be in control of my finances if only I just made more money,* you're not alone. But income alone isn't the answer. We've all seen examples of high-income earners drowning in debt and everyday individuals with modest earnings who manage to save, invest, and live comfortably. Do you know what sets them apart? Their habits.

In this chapter, we'll uncover why habits, not income, are the key to achieving financial freedom, long-term wealth, and peace of mind. You'll learn how to reduce financial stress, so you can enjoy life on your terms.

The Problem

- Cultural Messages about Spending vs. Saving

  Our culture encourages spending. Well-meaning friends will say "Treat yourself! You deserve it" or the often-used "You only live once!" (YOLO). Saving is often framed as deprivation. A chore, rather than a way of creating opportunities and freedom. As a result, even those with high incomes can find themselves living paycheck to paycheck, stressed about money.

- The Myth of Income

  It's easy to believe that if you made more money, your problems would be solved. However, financial security comes from how you manage your money, not how much you make. Without good habits, even a six-figure income can disappear as quickly as it arrives.

INTRODUCTION

> A Scarcity Mindset

Many people unknowingly operate from a scarcity mindset, focusing on what they don't have and what could go wrong. Adopting an abundance mindset, allows you to see money as a tool for creating possibilities, not just something to guard against loss.

> Emotional and Psychological Barriers

Money isn't just numbers. It's deeply tied to emotions. Fear, guilt, and shame around spending or saving can sabotage your financial success. Identifying these emotional blocks and shifting your mindset will free you to create better financial habits.

Case Study: Sarah and Tom

Sarah, a lawyer, earns $250,000 a year but spends as much as she makes, financing vacations and cars on credit. Tom, a teacher, earns $70,000 but lives well below his means. Through smart habits, Tom has invested consistently and grown his wealth to over a million dollars.

Sarah feels trapped, while Tom experiences peace of mind. This is proof that a large income doesn't equal financial security.

The Power of Habits

As James Clear explains in *Atomic Habits,* your habits are formed in loops, where a cue triggers an action that delivers a reward. Financial habits follow this same pattern.

For instance, consider the experience of receiving a paycheck. This moment serves as the cue, setting off a series of potential responses. You might respond with impulse spending, perhaps by treating yourself to a new gadget or accessory. In this case, the action is the impulse purchase, and the immediate reward is the temporary satisfaction and excitement of spending money on something that brings temporary happiness. However, this action may also lead to feelings of guilt later on, especially when you've overspent and undermined your budget.

INTRODUCTION

On the other hand, you might choose to save a portion of your paycheck, so the action shifts from impulsive spending to intentional saving and leads to a different reward: knowing you're contributing to your financial security or building an emergency fund. You reinforce the habit of saving, and create a positive feedback loop that encourages further saving in the future.

Becoming aware of these cues and the subsequent actions they trigger, modifies your responses to align better with your financial goals. For example, if you realize that you often indulge in impulse buys immediately after payday, you might implement a strategy such as setting up an automatic transfer to a savings account, which leads to the satisfaction of seeing your savings grow over time.

When you can identify other common cues in your financial behavior, such as emotional states or social situations, then you can alter them if you choose. For instance, if you notice you tend to use shopping as a coping mechanism when feeling stressed or anxious. Recognizing this cue can empower you to seek healthier alternatives for managing your emotions, like exercising or meditating.

Ultimately, these habit loops encourage financial habits that genuinely support your long-term goals, leading to greater financial stability and overall satisfaction.

I can help you work through and identify your spending or saving patterns, as well as your cues and triggers, so you can take the desired actions. As we identify your triggers and modify your actions, you create habits that serve your financial goals, and give you back control of your money.

The Power of Tiny Habits

You don't need to make huge changes overnight. Small financial habits like rounding up your savings or reviewing your expenses weekly, may seem insignificant at first but compound into major financial gains over time. Just as small drops fill a bucket, tiny changes add up to financial freedom.

INTRODUCTION

Habit Stacking

Habit stacking is a powerful way to anchor new habits to existing ones. Here are a couple of examples:

- After making coffee, transfer five dollars to your savings.
- After checking emails, log your expenses for the day.

Building habits into your routine makes managing your money automatic and stress-free.

The ABUNDANCE Habits

Throughout this book, I'll be using a framework called ABUNDANCE, which is a step-by-step system for building financial habits that create lasting wealth. This framework keeps you focused, motivated, and in control of your money, confirming your financial habits align with your values and helps you build a life of contentment, freedom, and sustainable wealth.

Each letter represents a key habit that works together to transform your financial life:

- **A**wareness

    Open your eyes to how your money flows, uncovering the habits, beliefs, and emotions that drive your financial decisions.

    You can't change what you don't recognize. Awareness is the first step to transformation.

- **B**alance

    Plan your spending with intention, so your lifestyle aligns with your values while securing your financial future.

    Balance gives you the freedom to enjoy today while building for tomorrow.

INTRODUCTION

- **U**nderstanding

    Clarity on exactly where your money goes can help you make informed decisions about spending, saving, and investing.

    Clarity reduces stress and puts you back in control of your financial choices.

- **N**otice

    Identify whether you're on or off track with your budget. By regularly checking in, you can adjust your behaviors to stay aligned with your financial goals.

    Small course corrections keep you moving steadily toward success.

- **D**isasters

    Create an emergency fund that gives you a safety net and protects you from inevitable unexpected expenses.

- **A**llocate

    Distribute your money through automation, so it flows effortlessly where it's needed, toward bills, savings, debt repayment, and investments, without relying on willpower.

    Automation makes staying on track easy, even when life gets busy.

- **N**avigate

    Borrow wisely, and pay down existing balances. When managed well, debt is a tool for growth.

    Navigate debt to your advantage by borrowing for growth, not consumption.

- **C**ompound

    Invest early and consistently to build wealth over time, and grow your money with minimal effort.

    The sooner you start, the more your wealth grows while you sleep.

➤ **E**valuate

Review, adjust, and celebrate your milestones to remain motivated.

Each step builds on the one before, creating momentum that transforms your relationship with money. With every habit you develop, you gain control, reduce financial anxiety, and grow your wealth.

Commit to Your Future

Set aside time each week to check in with yourself or with a partner about your finances. These sessions aren't about judgment but celebrating your progress and committing to your future. Small weekly steps keep you on track to creating an abundant you.

PART A

WHERE ARE YOU AT NOW?

CHAPTER

AWARENESS OF MONEY MINDSET

The first step on your ABUNDANCE path is **A**wareness, as your financial future is shaped more by your mindset than your income.

We often assume that more money will solve our financial problems, but the reality is that our mindset shapes our financial habits and outcomes. If you've ever felt stuck, stressed, or overwhelmed, it's not just the numbers but the beliefs driving your decisions. Becoming aware of your current money mindset is essential to achieving financial peace, freedom, and long-term wealth.

CHAPTER 1

SECTION 1
IDENTIFYING YOUR CURRENT MONEY BELIEFS

The Origins of Money Beliefs

Your beliefs about money don't appear out of thin air but are deeply rooted in various influences that shape your perspectives that were formed in childhood. You can't go back and change the past. You simply accept that you have one, and move on. These are some of the factors that shape your money philosophies.

- Family dynamics

    From an early age, the conversations you overhear, and the attitudes displayed by your family members, create a foundational framework for your understanding of money. Phrases like "We can't afford that" or "Money doesn't grow on trees" can instill a scarcity mindset, leading to view money as a limited resource rather than a tool for opportunity and growth.

    Families that promote open discussions about budgeting, saving, and investing can foster a more empowered attitude toward money. The emotional tone surrounding these discussions, for instance, fear or comfort, influences how you approach financial matters as an adult.

- Society and culture

    The broader societal context in which you live also plays a pivotal role in shaping your money beliefs. Media representations often glorify lavish lifestyles and consumption, sending the message that success and happiness are tied to spending. Advertisements and social media frequently celebrate material wealth while framing frugality as dull, boring, or outdated. This cultural narrative can pressure you to conform and lead to unhealthy spending habits that prioritize immediate gratification over long-term financial security, causing you to challenge and redefine your relationship with money.

> Personal experiences
Beyond familial and societal factors, personal financial experiences, both triumphs and setbacks, serve as powerful teachers. Achieving financial goals, such as successfully saving for a significant purchase or investing wisely, can boost your confidence and reinforce positive money habits. But experiencing setbacks can create fear and anxiety around money that leads to adopting defensive strategies that may hinder future growth.

These early influences leave a lasting imprint on your beliefs about money, forming patterns that can either empower you to pursue financial freedom or trap you in unhealthy financial behaviors. Identify and reflect on these origins to reshape your mindset and develop a healthier relationship with money that aligns with your values and aspirations.

Common Limiting Beliefs

Many people hold unconscious beliefs that block them from achieving financial success. Some common limiting beliefs include:

> "Money is the root of all evil."

> "I'm just not good with money."

> "I need to work harder to earn more."

> "Rich people are greedy."

These thoughts, even if subtle, shape your financial behavior. If you view money as something negative or unattainable, you'll subconsciously avoid it, even when opportunities arise. Recognizing and challenging these limiting beliefs is a crucial step toward creating a healthier relationship with money and achieving financial success. Coaching and self-reflection can be effective tools for overcoming these mental barriers.

Take a moment to identify if you have any current limiting beliefs about money.

CHAPTER 1

Here's a survey questionnaire based on beliefs that hold you back from achieving wealth. Each statement is designed to gauge your level of agreement on a scale from one to five, with one being "strongly disagree" and five being "strongly agree."

Wealth-Limiting Beliefs Survey

Instructions: Please read each statement carefully, and indicate your level of agreement by ticking the corresponding number.

Statement	1 (Strongly Disagree)	2 (Disagree)	3 (Neutral)	4 (Agree)	5 (Strongly Agree)
1. I don't deserve to be wealthy.					
2. Money is the root of all evil.					
3. I have to work hard for every penny.					
4. I'm not good with money.					
5. Wealth is only for the lucky or privileged.					
6. If I get rich, I will lose my friends or family.					
7. I'll never be able to save enough.					
8. I need to be in debt to be successful.					

9. Financial success means sacrificing my values.					
10. I have to choose between money and happiness.					
11. I don't have the skills or education to be wealthy.					
12. I will always struggle with money.					

Scoring instructions:

Add up the scores for each statement. Your total will range from twelve to sixty.

Here's how to interpret your score:

12–24: Low Limiting Beliefs

You have a healthy relationship with money and few limiting beliefs. You're likely to pursue wealth with confidence.

25–36: Moderate Limiting Beliefs

You may be holding onto some limiting beliefs. Consider exploring them further to improve your financial mindset.

37–48: High Limiting Beliefs

You hold several limiting beliefs about wealth that may be hindering your financial success. Consider strategies to challenge and reframe them.

49–60: Severe Limiting Beliefs

Your beliefs about money may significantly impact your ability to achieve wealth. Seek guidance to develop a healthier financial mindset.

CHAPTER 1

After completing the survey, you may find it helpful to engage in discussions or activities aimed at addressing the limiting beliefs identified in your scores. This could include journaling, coaching or therapy, and even financial education work-shops.

The Impact of Fear on Financial Decisions

Fear is one of the strongest drivers of poor financial decisions. Fear of failure can prevent you from investing and paralyze you, leaving you stuck in the same financial situation year after year, while fear of missing out (FOMO), can push you into spending impulsively. Here are some common fears:

- Fear of losing money

    Shying away from investing in any market due to the fear of losing your hard-earned money, causes you to miss out on the long-term benefits of investing, such as compound growth and wealth accumulation. Instead of participating in the market or the opportunity, you may choose to keep your funds in cash or low-risk investments, which often yield minimal returns. This conservative approach can hinder your ability to build substantial wealth over time.

- Fear of rejection

    You might be hesitant to negotiate your salary or ask for a raise due to fear of rejection or upsetting your employer, which results in accepting lower compensation than you deserve. Over time, this hesitance leads to stagnation, reducing your lifetime earnings and retirement savings.

- Fear of change

    The fear of change can prevent you from pursuing new job opportunities or career paths that may offer better financial prospects. Sticking to a familiar but unfulfilling job can limit your personal growth and potential income, as well as missed opportunities for advancement.

- Fear of failure

    The fear of failing can deter you from taking calculated risks necessary for growth, such as entrepreneurship opportunities or investing in ventures with high potential returns.

- Fear of financial literacy

    You might avoid seeking financial education due to fear of not understanding the more complex concepts or feeling overwhelmed by the information, which can cause reliance on others and a lack of confidence in making informed choices. As a result, you'll lose opportunities to grow your wealth through effective budgeting and calculated financial planning.

- Fear of judgment

    The fear of being judged by peers or family members can prevent you from seeking help or sharing your financial struggles, causing you to become isolated and unable to learn from the experience of others. Instead of exploring beneficial strategies or support systems, you remain stuck in harmful financial patterns.

- Fear of success

    The fear of success often stems from deep-seated beliefs and anxieties about financial success that includes increased responsibilities and anxiety over the possible loss of lifestyle and relationships. Opportunities are overlooked or avoided due to the discomfort associated with stepping out of your comfort zone. Ultimately, this fear of newfound wealth can create a cycle of being stuck, where the desire for financial stability is undermined by the very success that could provide it.

- Fear of the unknown

    The fear of the unknown can be a significant barrier to pursuing new financial opportunities, such as starting a business or investing in unfamiliar markets. This fear leads to sticking to familiar but less lucrative options and avoiding those who could give you greater wealth and financial security.

Take a moment to ask yourself which of these fears, if any, you've experienced.

CHAPTER 1

Case Study: Sarah

Sarah felt trapped in a cycle of financial insecurity. As a graphic designer, she was constantly stressed about money. Growing up, her parents' arguments over finances left a lasting impression. She would often hear them say things like, "We can't afford that," or "We're drowning in debt!" and her mother's worry, "I can't afford to be sick!"

These experiences led Sarah to subconsciously avoid saving. She internalized the belief that financial security was out of reach, so despite having a steady job, she felt inadequate and incapable of achieving it. She avoided saving and investing, which only contributed to her "stuck" feeling. Unaware of her negative, self-talk, she often wished for a better life. Her biggest dream, owning an investment property, seemed impossible on her low income.

The psychology of Sarah's transformation is rooted in shifting her mindset. She took action by reshaping her beliefs about money, beginning with identifying and journaling her negative thoughts and reframing them into positive affirmations. She challenged her limiting beliefs and followed a structured savings plan, before taking the leap to investing in shares.

As she learned more about personal finance, concepts like return on investment became less daunting, and she developed clear financial goals, holding herself accountable through regular check-ins. Her negative self-talk was replaced with a growth mindset, and she now thrives in a supportive online community that helps reduce her fears and keeps her on track.

Today, Sarah's financial situation has transformed dramatically. Within just two years, she bought her first investment property. She's learned to budget, track her expenses, and save more than she ever thought possible. Money stress is a thing of the past, as is her credit card debt. She now feels financially secure and is empowered with an additional income stream from freelance work, which boosted her savings even faster. Sarah no longer wakes up in the middle of the night with financial worries. She's in control of her money and knows she can achieve anything she sets her mind to.

SECTION 2
THE IMPACT OF MINDSET

Shaping Your Money Management

Your mindset profoundly impacts how you manage your money. It's the invisible hand that directs your financial choices. A scarcity mindset might lead you to be overly frugal, missing out on opportunities for growth, while a growth mindset allows you to see money as giving you greater confidence to further your education or start a side business.

When you change your thoughts about money, you change the way you save, spend, and grow it.

Psychological Barriers

Here are some common psychological blocks that hold people back:

- Perfectionism

    The desire to have everything perfect can delay taking action, whether it's creating a budget or starting an investment plan.

- Self-sabotage

    Believing you're undeserving of wealth causes poor decisions

- Social comparisons:

    Feelings of inadequacy means you're constantly comparing yourself to others' financial situations or lifestyles.

- Emotional spending

    Using shopping or spending as a coping mechanism for stress, anxiety, or unhappiness derails financial goals and creates cycles of debt.

- Fixed mindset

    Believing that financial abilities are static and can't be improved will stop you from seeking knowledge, learning new skills, or adapting to changing financial circumstances.

- Procrastination

    When you delay investing or saving due to fear of commitment and overwhelm, you endanger your financial future.

- Overwhelm

    Anxiety about making the wrong choice causes paralysis, meaning it stops you from making any decision at all.

- Analysis paralysis

    Feeling stuck as to which way to proceed, or not, stops many profitable projects from ever getting off the ground and brings about increased stress and a lack of progress.

Here are the steps I recommend for investors who find themselves stuck in analysis paralysis when evaluating a potential project. The DEVIL process can be used when you face indecision in any situation:

Five-Step DEVIL Technique

1. **D**eadline:

    Establish a specific timeframe for making your investment decision. This creates urgency and helps prevent endless deliberation.

2. **E**ssential

    Focus on the critical data necessary for your decision-making process. Avoid getting bogged down in excessive details that can cloud your judgment. Essential information *only*.

3. **V**isualize

    Picture the best outcome of your investment succeeding. Envisioning a positive result can help shift your mindset from fear of loss to excitement about potential gains.

4. **I**ncrements

    Take small steps to avoid overwhelm. Initiate action to break through the paralysis. Whether it's reaching out to a real estate agent or attending an open house, even a minor action can generate momentum.

5. **L**earn

    Always remember to review and adjust on your plan. Understand that your financial decisions can evolve. If your selected strategy or choice doesn't pan out as expected, don't hesitate to reassess and make necessary adjustments along the way.

Following these steps helps you make informed financial decisions with confidence.

CHAPTER 1

SECTION 3
SHIFTING TO A GROWTH-ORIENTED MONEY MINDSET

Changing Limiting Beliefs

To change your money mindset, you must first identify and challenge your beliefs. Ask yourself the following questions:

- What did I learn about money growing up?
- Do I believe I deserve wealth and financial freedom?
- How do I react emotionally when I spend, save, or invest?

Changing your limiting beliefs requires conscious effort and practice. Here's a practical exercise to help you identify and reframe limiting beliefs:

1. Write down your limiting beliefs about money, and question their validity. Ask yourself if there's evidence that contradicts these beliefs.

2. Once you've identified limiting beliefs, challenge them, and replace them with positive affirmations. For example, replace "I don't deserve to be wealthy" with "I'm worthy of financial success and abundance." Change "I'm not good with money" into "I'm learning how to manage my money better every day" or "Money is stressful" with "Money gives me choices."

AWARENESS OF MONEY MINDSET

Here's a table to help you identify and challenge some common limiting "money wound" beliefs. This structured approach allows you to articulate your beliefs, question their validity, and find evidence that contradicts them.

Limiting Belief	Challenge/ Question	Evidence to Contradict
I don't deserve to be wealthy.	Is it possible for money to be used for good?	Many charitable organizations and individuals use money to help others.
I'll never be financially secure.	What steps can I take to improve my financial situation?	People from various backgrounds have achieved financial stability through planning and effort.
I don't deserve to be wealthy.	Why do I feel I don't deserve wealth?	Everyone has the right to financial well-being; many deserving individuals achieve financial success.
Investing is too risky for me.	What information do I need to understand investing better?	Many people start investing with little knowledge and learn along the way; numerous resources are available.
I'm bad with money.	Can I identify specific instances where I made good financial decisions?	Many people have experienced setbacks but learned valuable lessons that improved their financial management.

I'll never get out of debt.	Have others successfully overcome debt? What did they do?	Countless stories of people paying off debt exist, often through budgeting and discipline.
I need to work harder to make more money.	Are there other ways to generate income besides working harder?	Passive income, investments, and side hustles are viable options that can generate revenue.
Wealthy people are greedy and selfish.	Do I know wealthy individuals who are generous and community-minded?	Many wealthy individuals contribute significantly to their communities through philanthropy and support.
I can't afford to save or invest.	What small amounts can I save or invest consistently?	Even small savings can add up over time; many financial plans advocate starting with minimal amounts.
Money is scarce and hard to come by.	Are there examples of people creating wealth in various ways?	Stories of entrepreneurship and innovation showcase how individuals have created financial success from nothing.

Instructions for Use:

Heal an old money-wound belief, with the ICE method, so you can recognize it as a story you've created to keep yourself unconsciously safe and within a familiar pattern.

> **I**dentify
> Write down any additional limiting beliefs you may have about money.

> **C**hallenge
> Use the questions to challenge each belief's validity.

> **E**vidence
> Provide evidence that contradicts the limiting belief, reinforcing the idea that they can be changed.

This small step of using the ICE method will raise your awareness and help you shift your mindset about money, leading to more empowering beliefs and healthier financial behaviors.

Shift from Fear to Confidence

Building confidence involves facing your fears and taking incremental steps toward financial growth:

> Educate yourself
> Knowledge reduces fear. Take financial literacy courses, or read books about personal finance.

> Set small goals
> Achieving small financial goals builds confidence and demonstrates that you can manage your money effectively. Do the small habit steps at the end of each chapter to improve your confidence, as you take back control of your money.

Moving from a Scarcity to a Growth Mindset

> Practice gratitude
> Regularly acknowledge and appreciate what you already have. It helps shift focus from what you lack and moves your personal energy to being more positive about many areas of your life, including money.

CHAPTER 1

If you find this challenging in regards to money, shift your awareness to another area in your life, and feel gratitude for that. For example, you may feel grateful that you have an abundance of fresh running water, food in your fridge, multiple clothes to wear each day, or a functioning body, all without any effort from you.

You could focus your gratitude on having a roof over your head and the many comforts in your life, or the nature surrounding you. Experiencing a feeling of abundance every day not only feels good but also attracts otherwise unseen opportunities to you.

Acknowledge even the smallest wins, like paying off a bill or saving an extra twenty dollars.

Try this daily gratitude exercise:

1. Take a few minutes daily to write down one thing you're grateful for regarding your financial situation.

2. Focus on progress, no matter how small. This rewires your brain to see money in a positive light.

➤ Embrace opportunities

View challenges as opportunities for growth rather than threats. This mindset encourages you to take calculated risks and pursue new avenues for financial advancement. When presented with a challenge, notice your language and thoughts. What do you say out loud to others and to yourself internally?

Remember to ask yourself an empowering question like "How could this be serving my personal growth?" Another powerful question to ask is "What would the person I'm becoming choose to do in this situation?"

➤ Visualization and Meditations

Visualization

Spend a few minutes each day visualizing your financial goals as if they're already achieved. Imagine yourself experiencing the emotions associated with success, and remember to take any inspired action that's aligned toward your goal.

Meditation

Incorporating a morning routine that includes a money meditation can profoundly influence your mindset and set the tone for the day ahead. Dedicating a few moments each morning to focus on your financial intentions creates a space for clarity and positive energy.

Visualize your financial goals, affirm your abundance, and enrich a mindset of prosperity. As you ground yourself in this intentional reflection, you develop a heightened awareness of your spending habits and decision-making throughout the day, which not only empowers you to make more informed choices, but also helps you approach challenges with confidence and a solution-oriented mindset.

Ultimately, starting your day with a money meditation aligns your thoughts and actions with your financial aspirations, setting you on a path toward achieving your goals with purpose and mindfulness.

Visualization for Anchoring Abundance

Meditation and visualization are powerful tools for grounding your thoughts in a mindset of abundance. To get into the right perspective, try the following visualization:

1. Find a quiet space.

2. Sit comfortably, and close your eyes, allowing your body to relax, and your mind to settle.

3. Picture a version of yourself who is confident, financially secure, and living life fully, free from stress.

4. Add vivid details. Immerse yourself in this image by engaging all of your senses. What do you see around you? Who is with you, and what are they saying? What are you wearing? Where are you? Pay attention to the tastes and smells. Perhaps you're enjoying a meal at your favorite restaurant. What flavor lingers in your mouth?

5. Consider the colors of your surroundings. Is it vibrant and lively or more subdued? Visualize this scene as a dynamic movie or a still photograph, whichever feels most vivid to you.

6. Embrace the emotions. Allow yourself to feel the sensations of peace, freedom, and security that come from knowing you have control over your finances. Imagine the joy and contentment as you pay for the meal, celebrating this moment together.

Make this a daily practice. Repeat this visualization each day to train your mind to embody the feelings of success and abundance you desire.

You can rewire your mindset and foster a deeper connection to the life you aspire to. When you've identified an area of money concern, recreate an ideal scene of how you would like it to play out instead. This is the fastest way to rewire your brain, as your subconscious mind simply accepts it as done, which anchors your thoughts to abundance.

Celebrate Small Wins

Building new habits takes time, and it's essential to celebrate small victories along the way. Whether it's saving fifty dollars, paying off a small debt, or setting up an automatic investment plan, acknowledge your progress. Rewards reinforce positive behavior and keep you motivated to continue building good habits.

Awareness of your thoughts is the first step to financial transformation. Understanding your money mindset, identifying limiting beliefs, and shifting to a growth-oriented approach, lays the foundation for a better financial future. In the next chapter, we'll look at designing a sustainable lifestyle that allows you to live below your means without sacrificing joy or freedom.

Now, let's dive in and plan your spending with intention!

WEEK 1
SMALL STEPS TO THE FUTURE ABUNDANT YOU

- Complete the money beliefs survey.

  Reflect on your beliefs about money by filling out the money-beliefs survey. This will help you uncover any hidden thoughts or habits that may be influencing your financial behavior, giving you the clarity to make positive changes.

- Observe your inner dialogue.

  Pay attention when there's negative self-talk or limiting thoughts about money. Each time you catch a negative thought, pause and reframe it on the spot into a more empowering belief. For example, replace "I'll never be good with money" with "I am learning how to improve my financial skills every day."

- Celebrate every reframe.

  Reinforce positive change by celebrating each time you successfully reframe a negative thought. Give yourself a victory gesture, like a fist pump. Each celebration rewires your brain to associate success with progress.

CHAPTER

BALANCE

Plan Spending with Intention.

Imagine owning everything you need and never worrying about debt. Does that sound like freedom to you?

Many people associate spending less with sacrifice or deprivation, but the truth is that living below your means is the ultimate form of financial freedom. When your lifestyle costs less than you earn, you gain the ability to save, invest, and make decisions without fear. It's not about cutting out joy but the habit of intentional living. Let's explore how this habit of underspending can unlock peace of mind, the freedom to focus on what matters, and long-term financial security.

CHAPTER 2

SECTION 1
THE POWER OF INTENTIONAL LIVING

Aligning Spending with Values

The key to underspending without feeling deprived is to spend intentionally. Instead of focusing on what you can't buy, align your spending with what truly matters to you. Ask yourself if it reflects your values or brings you joy.

When your spending reflects your priorities, you're less likely to feel the need to compensate with impulse buys.

Wants vs. Needs

Learn to differentiate between wants and needs. If it isn't something essential like housing, food, or transportation, it's a want, such as having expensive food delivered. This doesn't mean cutting out all your wants but prioritizing and being thoughtful about when and how you indulge.

SECTION 2
THE PSYCHOLOGY OF MONEY

Lifestyle Creep

It's a common trap that when your income increases, so do your expenses. This is called lifestyle creep, the tendency to upgrade your lifestyle as your earnings grow. New clothes and fancier cars seem justified, because you're making more. But without discipline, you'll be trapped in a cycle of spending, preventing you from building long-term wealth.

Emotional Triggers

Spending isn't just logical, it's emotional. Advertisers know this, which is why they create ads that make you feel excitement and envy. Recognizing the emotional triggers behind your spending can help you take back control.

Do you buy things when you're lonely, stressed, or bored? When you find out about a sale, do you get excited about a great deal, even if you don't need the item?

Awareness Exercise

Take a moment to reflect on your recent purchases. The aim here is to identify any patterns as you reflect: What emotions were you feeling *before* the purchase? Was it planned? Did you feel satisfaction or regret it afterward?

Use the word *CREDIT* as an acronym related to the six habit steps. Select a specific habit you want to examine. This could be financial, such as impulse spending, or any other area of your life that you feel could use improvement.

CHAPTER 2

➤ **C**ue.

Identify the cues or triggers that lead to your financial habits, and write them down.

Consider time of day, location, emotional state, such as stress, boredom, or happiness, and social triggers, such as people or situations that influence you.

For example:

- ✓ I get bored in the evenings and wind up shopping online. (time of day).
- ✓ I walk by a store I love on my way home (location).
- ✓ I feel stressed after a long workday, and I relax by shopping. (emotional state).

➤ **R**ecognize

Look at your actions, and outline how you react to the cues. Be as detailed as possible. For example:

- ✓ After checking my bank balance and seeing a surplus, I immediately go shopping.
- ✓ After receiving an email about new arrivals at my favorite store, I click the link.
- ✓ When I feel down, I buy something to make myself feel better.

➤ **E**valuate

Determine the immediate rewards, their effect on your motivation to repeat the habit, and the long-term consequences of your actions. For example:

- ✓ I feel a temporary rush of excitement from buying something new (immediate reward).
- ✓ I enjoy the experience of shopping, which distracts me from my stress (immediate reward).

- ✓ I often feel guilt or regret when I see my bank balance decrease (long-term consequence).

➤ **D**ecide.

Now that you've mapped out the cues, actions, and rewards associated with your habit, take a moment to reflect, and make a decision about the following.

- ✓ Does the immediate satisfaction outweigh any negative consequences?
- ✓ How can I alter my behavior in response to the cues?

    For example, doing something else you enjoy, like taking a walk with a friend or engaging in your hobby.

    If a specific location triggers your habit, how can you modify your surroundings to reduce temptation? Identify healthier, more fulfilling rewards that align with your goals.

➤ **I**mplement

What are some improved actions you can take to replace the old ones?

Based on your decisions, create an actionable plan for implementing changes that align with your long-term desired reality. Set specific, measurable goals that incorporate new cues, actions, and rewards.

- ✓ New cue

    When I receive my paycheck, I will automatically transfer a portion to savings.

- ✓ New action

    Instead of shopping, I will allocate thirty minutes to exercise or engage in a creative hobby.

- ✓ New reward

    I'll treat myself to a small reward each month when I meet my savings goal.

CHAPTER 2

> **T**rack

    Establish goals, and monitor your progress to ensure effective habit changes.

By following this exercise, you will gain a deeper understanding of your habits and begin reshaping them to align with your financial goals. Remember, change takes time and practice, so be patient with yourself, as you implement these new strategies! And make sure you always reward yourself for each small step of achievement along the way. This is positive reinforcement. Recognizing your triggers will help you pause and reconsider the next time you feel the urge to spend impulsively.

How to Sustain Your Healthy Habits

Acknowledging and celebrating your achievements and successes along the way to financial freedom is a powerful habit for creating lasting, long-term change. It reinforces positive behavior and boosts motivation. I want you to embrace this habit, internalize it, and make it a cornerstone of your financial transformation. Discovering ways to reward yourself and celebrate your wins will help you maintain your motivation, and stay committed to achieving your ultimate goal.

> Create reward systems.

    Did you know, according to Experian, the average total consumer household debt in 2023 was $104,215? That's up eleven percent from 2020, when average total consumer debt was $92,727. This means that paying off debt is a huge achievement, so you must remember to celebrate your progress, such as making the final payment on a credit card or paying off your car loan. You could throw a debt-free party, enjoy a special (non-monetary) reward, or simply take a moment to reflect just how far you've come. I know I say this a lot, but it bears repeating: The habit of celebrating milestones keeps you motivated and reinforces positive financial habits.

    Living below your means isn't about eliminating joy but rewarding yourself in meaningful and (mostly) non-monetary ways. Use these small, medium, and larger rewards to celebrate different levels of milestone achievements along your financial journey:

- ✓ Small rewards (daily and weekly)

    Enjoy a peaceful walk in nature, read a favorite book, or take a quiet moment to unwind and reflect.

- ✓ Medium rewards (monthly)

    Treat yourself to a day off or a fun activity. After hitting a savings milestone, you might host a game night or movie marathon with friends, take an afternoon off for a creative project, or enjoy a relaxing home spa day.

- ✓ Larger rewards (yearly)

    After a major financial milestone like paying off a debt, dedicate time to a passion project, plan a vacation or make a meaningful purchase.

Creating a reward system not only keeps you motivated but also aligns with your goal of financial freedom by reinforcing connection and intentional living without too much extra spending.

- ➤ Seek reinforcement

    You don't have to go it alone. Joining communities focused on frugal living or intentional spending can provide both inspiration and accountability. Look for online groups and local meetups. You can even do challenges like "No-Spend" months to help you stay motivated and connected to like-minded people.

Now that you understand how to spend your money with intention, you need to identify exactly where your money goes, so you have a clear picture of your current financial situation. This is where the real fun begins, because tracking your money isn't about restriction, it's about creating freedom.

Let's dive in and start building the wealth you deserve.

CHAPTER 2

WEEK 2
SMALL STEPS TO THE FUTURE ABUNDANT YOU

- Identify your emotional spending triggers.
  - ✓ Use the CREDIT process. During the week, pay attention to situations or emotions that lead to any money habit you'd like to adjust, like impulse spending.
  - ✓ Write down any patterns you notice, such as boredom, stress, or excitement, so you can become more aware, and take control of your financial decisions.
- Design a personalized rewards system.
  - ✓ Create a tiered rewards system to celebrate your financial progress. Assign different reward levels based on the size and impact of each new habit that you create. Remember to include both monetary and non-monetary rewards.
- Accumulate three consecutive habit-stacking days.

Were you able to accumulate three consecutive days of habit stacking? If not, try this exercise: Go a full three days (seventy-two hours) without negative thoughts or self-talk about money. If a negative thought slips in, don't worry, just reset the clock, and start again. The goal is to train your mind to focus on empowering beliefs. Yes, it's possible, and it does take time. Keep going, until you complete three full days, and notice how it shifts your mindset.

PART B

WHERE EXACTLY DOES YOUR MONEY GO?

CHAPTER

UNDERSTANDING IS POWER

Do you know where your money goes?

One cup of coffee per day is just four dollars, but over a year, that's $1,460. It's easy to overlook small expenses, but over time, they can silently drain your finances. This chapter is about gaining an understanding, because you can't change what you don't know. Knowing your starting point and where your money goes, gives you control, reduces anxiety, and helps you align your spending with what matters most.

CHAPTER 3

SECTION 1
WHY KNOWING YOUR NUMBERS MATTERS

Drawing a financial line in the sand is a crucial step toward achieving financial empowerment and security. Where are you now? Do you have multiple loans? Student debts? Credit cards at their limit? No matter where you are, by clearly defining your current financial starting point, you set the stage for making informed decisions and establishing achievable goals.

Understanding where you stand allows you to identify areas for improvement, whether it's managing debt, increasing savings, or investing wisely. It gives you a sense of control and motivation, so you can take proactive steps, and prioritize your financial commitments for the future, while uncovering areas where you can save or invest.

Every successful financial journey is a series of small steps, and knowing your personal situation is that next phase. It's not just about tracking what you have, but knowing your financial story and using that knowledge to create a brighter, more secure future. So no matter where you start from or how bad you may feel your situation is, embrace this opportunity to transform your relationship with money, and take charge of your financial destiny!

Let's understand exactly where you are now.

Create a comprehensive snapshot of your current financial situation. This will give you focus as to where to direct your money in the future, so that you make it work for you.

Instructions

1. Make a chart as shown below.
2. Fill in all your current loans or outstanding debts. This includes
   - the current interest rate you're being charged
   - the amount you're required to pay each month
   - when that payment is due
3. Put the smaller debts on the right, and the larger debts on the left.

Remember that this table is for your eyes only. It's not about feeling any guilt or embarrassment, but taking charge of your current situation, and doing so creates total understanding.

My Personal Financial Snapshot

	Larger Debt: Loans			Smaller Debt: Loans			
	Investment property loan	Business loan	Home loan (primary residence)	Student loan	Personal loan	Credit card	Cash owed to a friend
Total balance owning							
Interest rate							
Monthly payment							
Due date							

Now that you know where you currently stand, let's take a look at the habits that helped you get here.

CHAPTER 3

The Psychology of Unconscious Spending

Unconscious spending occurs when purchases feel automatic and habitual, often driven by convenience or emotional triggers, rather than thoughtful decision-making. For instance, swiping your card for a quick coffee on the way to work or opting for takeout when you're feeling exhausted, can become routine actions you don't think twice about. These seemingly insignificant transactions may seem harmless in isolation, but they can quickly accumulate, leading to significant financial strain over time.

Without paying attention, it's easy to overlook how often these small expenses add up, creating a sense of financial stress that can catch you off guard. Bringing awareness to your spending habits empowers you to make more intentional choices. This newfound mindfulness allows you to assess where your money is going, prioritize your needs, and identify areas where you can cut back, ultimately leading to greater control over your finances and a reduction in stress.

The Power of Small Changes

Big financial transformations aren't immediate but happen through small, consistent changes. Here are a few examples of what you might consider to help create more savings:

- Cancel unused subscriptions

    Review monthly subscriptions like streaming services or gym memberships, and cancel those you don't use.

- Cook at home

    Meal prep, and cooking at home, rather than dining out or ordering in from DoorDash or UberEATS, where they not only charge more for the food but put a service charge on top of that. Try new recipes to make it enjoyable.

- Limit impulse purchases

    Implement a waiting period. Even waiting twenty-four hours before making non-essential purchases will make a difference.

UNDERSTANDING IS POWER

- Use public transportation

    Save on fuel and parking by using public transit, biking, or walking when possible.

- Shop with a list

    Make a shopping list before going to the grocery store to avoid buying unnecessary items. It may be difficult, but stick to your list, as a few extra items here and there can really add up, and they're usually items you wanted instead of needed.

    Also, many stores that also sell groceries now have a subscription service, where you can get food delivered to your doorstep with no delivery charge, which helps avoid impulse buying and purchasing items you're sure you're out of, when in fact you have five of them.

- Buy generic brands

    Opt for the store brand or generic products, which are often cheaper and just as good.

- Cut utility costs

    Be mindful of energy consumption by turning off lights, using energy-efficient appliances, and lowering or raising the thermostat as needed.

- Limit entertainment expenses

    Look for free or low-cost community events instead of expensive outings. Consider hosting game nights or potlucks.

- Use coupons and discounts

    Take advantage of coupons, cash-back apps, and promotional discounts when shopping.

- Reduce coffee shop visits

    Brew coffee at home. You can even use the same syrups the coffee shops do, and you'll still save money.

> Evaluate your insurance policies

   Shop around for better rates on car, home, and health insurance, and consider bundling policies for savings.

> Negotiate bills

   Contact service providers to negotiate lower rates on internet, cable, and phone bills.

> Limit alcohol and tobacco

   Cutting back on alcohol and smoking can significantly reduce your spending.

> Buy in bulk

   Purchase nonperishable items in bulk to save money over time, but ensure it's for items you use regularly.

> Avoid retail therapy

   Find alternative ways of coping with stress or boredom that don't involve shopping.

> Participate in a buy-nothing group

   Join local groups where you can give away and receive items for free instead of buying new.

> Plan vacations wisely

   Look for off-peak travel times, and consider staycations or camping to save on vacation costs.

> Review your phone plan

   Evaluate your mobile phone plan, and switch to a less expensive one if you're not utilizing all your data or features.

Applying just a few of these minor adjustments consistently, can have a big impact on your financial future. Redirecting these small savings into an investment will also help grow your wealth effortlessly over time.

UNDERSTANDING IS POWER

SECTION 2
FINANCIAL TRACKING

Tracking your income and expenses isn't about restriction but empowerment. When you know exactly where your money goes, you gain the ability to make conscious choices. Are your expenses aligned with your values? Are you spending on what brings joy and meaning? Tracking answers these questions, and helps you redirect your money to what matters most.

Check out your credit card or bank statement, and examine your spending habits closely with an objective mindset, as if you're an observer, and try to identify any recurring patterns in your expenditures. Use the CREDIT process, and consider factors such as the days of the week you might overspend, the types of items you purchase, such as clothing, technology, and entertainment, and the times of day when you make these purchases. Reflect on what this information reveals about your spending habits, and how they may be influencing your financial situation.

Case Study: Kuma Wants His Own Home

When I first transferred to Sydney with Westpac, I often met up with some old friends from Dubbo who were also living in the big smoke. Our Friday night gatherings at a lively inner-city pub became a weekly ritual, offering a much-needed break from the weekly grind.

It was during one of these evenings that I met Kumarisen(Kuma), a friend of a friend. Over a few months, we all grew close, and during one of our conversations about finances, Kuma was surprised to learns that despite earning three times my salary, he had no savings to show for it, while I'd recently managed to purchase my first home in Rose Bay. To him, it just didn't add up.

Curious, I asked if he was willing to do whatever it took to save for a house deposit. When he agreed, I handed him a small pocket-sized spiral notebook and suggested he jot down every single expense he made throughout the week. Each Friday night, as part of our usual pub meet-ups but before the drinks were flowing, we'd sit down and go through his list. Within a month, his spending patterns revealed themselves clearly. For the first time, Kuma truly understood where his money was going.

Armed with this new awareness, he focused on tracking his expenses consistently and made a few strategic adjustments. One major change was how we spent our Fridays. Kuma needed to unwind after a hectic workweek, as we all did, and socializing was his way of doing that. So, instead of hitting the pubs, we began hosting game nights at each other's homes. The laughter, connection, and fun remained, but the cost dropped significantly, which was his focus. It allowed him to balance both his need for social connection, and his goal of saving for a house deposit.

One Friday, as we were reviewing his expenses, I got a little frustrated with him for not tracking a certain expense properly when he listed a larger charge under "other." He simply smiled and said 'Okay, Okay, I'll do it better next time!'. Later, we both laughed at his sneaky move, as he surprised me with the most beautiful flowers I'd ever received. It was his heartfelt thank you for helping him get clarity on his financial goals, and understanding the difference between his wants and needs.

In less than a year, with continued diligence and smarter spending choices, Kuma achieved his goal and saved enough to purchase his home in Mount Colah, NSW, all while still having fun with his friends.

Low-Tech Tracking Solutions

There are multiple ways to track your spending. The key is to choose a method that works best for you and your lifestyle. Here are a few options to consider:

- Budgeting apps and spreadsheets

    Apps like ASIC's MoneySmart make tracking expenses easy by categorizing your spending and providing monthly summaries.

    Spreadsheets are another excellent option if you prefer a more customized approach. You can create your own budget template to suit your financial goals.

- Pen-and-paper tracking systems

    For those who prefer simplicity, a notebook or journal can work just as well. Write down every expense, no matter how small, and review it at the end of the day. This manual method builds awareness, and keeps you engaged with your finances.

- Daily, weekly, and monthly check-ins

    - ✓ Daily check-ins

        Review your spending at the end of each day.

    - ✓ Weekly reviews

        Look at your spending trends, and adjust where needed.

    - ✓ Monthly summaries

        Assess how well your spending aligns with your financial goals.

The more consistent you are, and the more often you do this, the easier it becomes to spot patterns, and make adjustments.

Daily Habit Tracking

- Habit Stacking

    The easiest way to build a new habit is by attaching it to an existing one, a concept known as habit stacking. For example, while sipping your morning coffee, take five minutes to log your expenses from the previous day. This small act, repeated daily, becomes second nature over time.

- Automate where possible

    Reduce friction by automating parts of the process. Use bank summaries or credit card reports to track spending categories effortlessly. Many apps allow you to sync accounts, so your transactions are recorded automatically.

CHAPTER 3

➤ Celebrate small wins

Tracking every expense can feel tedious at first, so again, celebrate your progress along the way. Each time you reach a tracking milestone like completing a full week or month, give yourself a small or medium reward, whichever is more suitable. This positive reinforcement keeps you motivated, and makes tracking an enjoyable part of your routine.

Tracking and understanding your regular expenses gives you the clarity and control to make better financial decisions on a daily, weekly, and monthly basis. Now that you know where your money goes, it's time to create a budget, and notice when you're on or off track.

Let's now create a budget that helps you thrive, not just survive.

WEEK 3

SMALL STEPS TO THE FUTURE ABUNDANT YOU

- ➤ Get clear on your financial snapshot.

    Take stock of your current financial situation by listing your outstanding loans, credit card balances, and any other debts you may have. Knowing your starting point is essential for tracking progress.

- ➤ Identify your current spending habits.

    Use your bank statements to help you identify patterns and areas where you can make adjustments that align with your financial goals.

- ➤ Choose your tracking method.

    Set up your preferred system for tracking your finances, whether it's an app, spreadsheet, or a pen-and-paper method. Pick the tool that works best for your lifestyle and is easy to maintain.

- ➤ Schedule a daily or weekly review.

    Commit to a specific time of day and time for reviewing your finances. Block it off on your calendar, so it becomes a consistent part of your routine.

CHAPTER

NOTICE - WHEN ON OR OFF BUDGET

A budget isn't a punishment. It's a plan for achieving your dreams.

After reviewing thousands of my customers' personal situations during my time working at a bank, I noticed a clear pattern. As humans, we often feel stressed and anxious when we can't easily pay for something we consider an emergency, which can trigger a financial crisis. The truth is, we need to afford our everyday expenses, but beyond that, most of us also desire the ability to enjoy life. We want enough money for things like vacations, nice cars or furniture, or to indulge in hobbies. Financial security is a driving force for many, and we don't like the feeling of missing out on experiences that bring us joy or make us feel successful.

CHAPTER 4

At our core, we're all wired to seek comfort and stability, and this includes our finances. We have a natural tendency to avoid discomfort, which can lead to procrastination when it comes to saving or budgeting. We also have a deep desire for control, and when we're having money troubles, it heightens our stress. But there's also the instinct to prioritize short-term rewards like buying something new or going on an impulse shopping spree, over long-term financial health. We value immediate gratification and put off the discomfort of planning for the future. Yet, at the same time, we also crave a sense of security and accomplishment. Balancing these conflicting desires is at the heart of many financial struggles.

Let me be upfront: I personally *hate* budgeting, but I still do it. Why? Because having a budget means freedom. The good news is, you only need to create your budget once. After that, it becomes a guide for achieving your financial goals without constantly worrying about every dollar. Let's walk through why budgeting is the foundation for financial peace, and how to build a plan that works for you.

SECTION 1
WHY BUDGETS GIVE YOU FREEDOM

- Budgets Give You Permission to Spend Guilt-Free

  A budget isn't about saying "no" to everything you enjoy. It's about giving yourself permission to spend on what matters without guilt or anxiety. When you know exactly how much you've set aside for living expenses, savings, and splurges, you can enjoy life without second-guessing every purchase.

- You Can Achieve Both Small and Large Goals

  Your budget serves as a road map to your dreams, helping you meet short-term goals like vacations and long-term goals like paying off debts or buying a house. Budgeting makes it possible to get there without sacrificing peace of mind.

Case Study: Budgeting the Family Vacation

The Grangers, a hardworking family of four, had always dreamed of taking their kids to Disney World, but they were determined not to fall into the trap of using credit cards to finance the trip. They'd seen firsthand how credit card debt could snowball, especially with interest piling up on the balance long after the trip was over. They didn't want to come home from their dream holiday, only to face months of paying off the debt that came with it.

So, they decided to take a different approach. A full year before their planned trip, they sat down together to create a detailed vacation budget. They figured out the total cost, including flights, accommodation, park tickets, food, and souvenirs.

CHAPTER 4

They divided the total amount by twelve, setting aside a small, manageable amount each month. Then they opened a dedicated savings account they nicknamed *Lets Do Disney*, ensuring the money was separate from their regular savings and expenses.

The key to their success was staying committed. The Grangers tracked their progress each month, watching their vacation fund grow steadily. They celebrated small milestones along the way, which not only kept them motivated but also reinforced the importance of delayed gratification. As the year progressed, they found they didn't have to make drastic sacrifices. By only cutting back on small, non-essential purchases, they were able to save without feeling deprived.

When the time finally came, the family was able to pay for their entire vacation in full, without relying on credit cards. They arrived at Disney World excited and stress-free, knowing that everything was already paid for. Their dream vacation became a reality, and when they returned home, they didn't have any lingering financial worries to deal with. The trip was exactly what they'd hoped for, accumulating memories without the weight of debt hanging over them.

The Grangers realized that by budgeting and planning ahead, they not only created the holiday of a lifetime but also built the financial confidence to manage their future goals with the same level of success.

SECTION 2
BUILDING YOUR FIRST AND ONLY BUDGET

Establishing this system frees you from the need to depend solely on willpower or control. Baumeister, an American social psychologist, articulated this concept beautifully through his research, where he says willpower functions like a muscle that can become fatigued through overuse, because it's a finite resource. Those who succeed don't have more willpower than you. They just cultivate better routines and habits that eventually become automatic. This means fewer daily decisions need to be made, which in turn requires less active thought, and therefore less conscious effort or mental energy. And isn't that a great goal to have with your money?

The beauty of this budgeting method is that you only need to create it once. After that, the system pretty much runs itself with a minimal amount of effort on your part. Focus is only required during your monthly and annual review when you notice any needed adjustments.

Saving vs. Spending

Saving for your goals is crucial for achieving financial wellness. Strategically planning and directing your money will assist you in achieving your savings objectives while allowing for enjoyment in your current spending. This budgeting strategy emphasizes finding a balance between saving and spending. You can direct your monthly savings toward a single goal, like building an emergency fund, or divide it among several objectives, such as contributing to a retirement account and saving for your home or investment property. Whatever your goal or focus, having a savings target is essential.

CHAPTER 4

The DEAL Method

A great way to remember how to allocate your budget is to break it down into portions for different categories, which can be summed up with the DEAL method. It taps into core aspects of human psychology, helping to create a financial plan that aligns with your deepest needs and desires.

> **D**isaster/**D**ebt
>
> Life is unpredictable, and unexpected events will inevitably happen. Whether it's a medical emergency, a car breakdown, or a sudden job loss, disasters are part of the human experience. The psychological challenge here is that we have a natural tendency to avoid discomfort and uncertainty. However, acknowledging that these events will occur and preparing for them, allows you to regain a sense of control and security when things go wrong. It's not about expecting the worst but creating a safety net that gives you peace of mind in turbulent times.
>
> And after preparing for those inevitable Disasters, managing Debt is an equally important part of financial security. High-interest debt in particular can feel like a constant weight on your shoulders. Psychologically, it triggers stress, guilt, and a sense of being trapped, all of which can undermine your financial and emotional well-being.
>
> You may avoid confronting it, hoping it will go away on its own, but ignoring it only makes the problem worse. Paying off debt as quickly as possible gives you back control over your finances, which reduces stress and creates space for future opportunities.
>
> Your natural desire for freedom and security can only be fully realized when you no longer carry the burden of unpaid debts. By prioritizing debt repayment, you reduce the financial strain that holds you back from pursuing our aspirations and enjoying life's luxuries. The sooner you take action, the quicker you can move toward financial independence.

> **E**veryday Expenses
>
> Everyday expenses are the unavoidable essential costs of living. From rent or mortgage payments, to groceries, utilities, and transportation, these are the basic needs that sustain us.

There's also an element of non-essential everyday spending, like eating out or entertainment, that makes life enjoyable. Psychologically, people seek stability and comfort, and budgeting for these everyday needs means you don't fall into the trap of overspending or worrying about the basics. It helps you feel grounded, secure, and capable of managing your daily life without constant stress.

- **A**spire

    Your goals, both short-and long-term, represent the things you strive for in life, such as homeownership, saving for a child's education, or a comfortable retirement. But aspirations go beyond just financial stability. Psychologically, there's a deep need for connection and meaningful experiences that bring us closer to others, like creating memorable celebrations, with lots of love, laughter, and shared joy, reinforcing the importance of setting aside resources for the things that truly matter.

    Or perhaps you'd just love to explore foreign countries, experiencing different cultures or taking a well-earned break to recharge. These goals aren't just about the material rewards but enriching your life while fueling your passions and enriching your personal growth.

    At our core, we all need purpose and direction. Setting these types of goals regarding financial stability, connection, or adventure, provides a roadmap for your life. You want to feel like you're moving toward something meaningful, knowing that your actions align with your values and long-term vision. Financial goals give you a sense of motivation and fulfillment, as you actively work to create the life you've always dreamed of.

    So, take time to ask yourself what makes you feel safe and secure. What brings you connection and excitement? These are the questions that shape your aspirations and fuel your goals.

- **L**uxuries

    Life isn't just about surviving but thriving and really enjoying the everyday moments. Luxuries are non-essential but deeply satisfying. Having these luxuries allows you to experience fulfillment and happiness.

CHAPTER 4

The challenge is balancing your desire for immediate gratification with long-term financial security. Budgeting for luxuries means enjoying life now without guilt or feeling like you're missing out, while still being responsible with your financial planning.

Using the DEAL method addresses the full spectrum of human needs and desires. It means you're prepared for the inevitable while also appreciating the simple pleasures that make life worthwhile. This holistic approach to budgeting aligns with the psychological drivers that influence spending habits.

The 60/20/10/10 DEAL Rule

Take your monthly after-tax income, and distribute it into four categories.

1. Allocate Sixty Percent to Expenses

    Sixty percent of your after-tax monthly income goes to regular expenses, which are essential costs that typically remain consistent each month and for some discretionary spending. You do this by multiplying your after-tax monthly income by 0.6 or typing in your income amountX60% on a calculator.

    Fixed expenses include

    - rent or mortgage payment,
    - car payment or public transportation
    - utilities (electricity, water, gas, internet)
    - phone bill
    - groceries
    - insurance.

    Flexible discretionary spending includes

    - dining out
    - shopping for clothes,

- vacations
- entertainment
- hobbies
- gym memberships.

These are expenses that aren't strictly necessary but are important to your lifestyle.

If the total exceeds sixty percent of your income, consider strategies to reduce costs. The easiest to reduce are the items on the discretionary spending list, such as entertainment, socializing, dining out, and clothes shopping. It might be time to reassess your priorities. Consider which expenses are truly important to you and which could be trimmed to boost your savings.

You might then look for savings at the grocery store, find ways to cut down on energy or water consumption, or consider moving to a more affordable living situation to help reduce the total amount spent in the fixed expenses.

2. Allocate Twenty Percent for Disasters and Debt Reduction

   The most common form of financial stress is unexpected bills. So, the first step is having funds set aside for these emergencies. Once you have at least three months saved, direct this money into debt reduction, which means paying off credit cards or personal/home loans quicker.

   Since everyone's financial path is unique, you'll have the power to decide exactly where to focus this portion, giving you ultimate control to achieve your financial goals.

   After working with thousands of people seeking to organize their finances, I've found this is the most commonly recommended order for debt prioritization.

   - Credit card(s)
   - Personal loan(s)
   - Home loan(s) and student loans.

3. Allocate Ten Percent for Saving Aspirations

   This category is all about achieving your financial targets, such as the long-term goal of saving for retirement, or a short-term goal of a car or holiday.

   If you notice that saving ten percent of your current income each month isn't feasible, don't be discouraged. Instead, establish a savings goal that aligns with your personal circumstances. Even setting aside a hundred dollars a month is a positive step. Saving something is always better than saving nothing. Always!

   If you're focused on paying down high-interest debts, you might want to adjust this plan to allocate a larger portion of your budget toward those repayments. Prioritizing high-interest debts can help you become financially secure quicker.

4. Allocate Ten Percent for Luxuries and Fun

   This is where you get to enjoy your life. Spend this money guilt-free on any luxury items you choose, splurge and have some fun.

This framework serves as a general guideline. You may need to adjust these percentages slightly based on your unique financial situations, goals, and obligations. Set it up once, and then check what's needed to make it work for you. For example, if you're living in a high-cost area, you may need to allocate more than sixty percent of your take-home income to essential expenses, while being focused on aggressive debt repayment might increase the percentage designated toward that. If you're unsure as to your own requirements, I suggest that you start with the guideline of 60/20/10/10, and see if you need to adjust the percentage up or down. But do this only if needed at your monthly review.

Short-Term Goal: Get Control of Your Money

Back in my day, managing money often involved a simple yet effective system of envelopes. Yes, I'm old. Microwaves weren't even invented yet!

Anyway, each envelope was designated for a specific category of expenses, such as groceries, rent, utilities, and entertainment. At the beginning of each month, we would take our cash out of the yellow payee envelope, and divide it among these other envelopes according to our budget. This hands-on approach not only helped us visually track our spending but also instilled a sense of discipline and accountability. Once an envelope was empty, that was it for the month, so we had to prioritize our needs, and make conscious choices about how we allocated our resources. There was a certain satisfaction in physically handling money, knowing exactly where it was going, and feeling the immediate impact of our financial decisions. In a world without digital banking and credit cards, this method fostered a deep understanding of budgeting and encouraged us to live within our means. It was a straightforward, tactile way of managing finances that many found effective and reliable.

So, how do we get control of our money today? By setting up five bank accounts. And like the envelopes, each one has a very specific purpose of working to achieve financial freedom.

Transaction Fees: Wayne's Story

When I purchased my home in Tempe, Sydney, I had a spare room that I decided to rent out to help pay down the mortgage faster. One of the applicants for the room was Wayne. As part of the application process, I reviewed his bank statements and noticed that although he could easily afford the rent, his spending habits were costing him unnecessarily, because he frequently used 'other' banks' ATMs to withdraw cash, paying a $2.50 fee per transaction *every single time*. He made these withdrawals multiple times a day for lunch, dinner, and even drinks after work.

When Wayne moved in, I saw an opportunity to help him change some of these habits. We worked together to set up bank accounts with specific purposes: one for emergencies, one for everyday expenses, another for savings/aspirations, and one for his splurge or luxury money. A fifth bank account wasn't necessary, as he had no credit card debt at the time. Instead of withdrawing cash for every small expense, we changed the system to allow just one withdrawal per week for his cash spending. This alone saved him a significant amount in bank fees. In fact, it came out to almost half of his rent! By setting up these purposeful accounts and cutting out unnecessary fees, Wayne was able to better manage his money, and I was happy to have helped him take control of his finances and be confident in his ability to pay his rent.

CHAPTER 4

I spent thirteen years working for a bank, where my main job was to encourage customers to open multiple accounts with them, enabling the bank to charge account keeping fees. It's a key strategy for how banks generate substantial profits. Did you know they earn billions every year? This highlights the importance of finding ways to reduce your bank fees. By doing so, you could save hundreds of dollars each year, keeping that money in your account instead of contributing to the bank's profits!

Rather than opening just any bank account in the four major Australian banks, do a Google search for fee-free banking options. You will need to select two banks, one for your primary transaction accounts and the second for your emergency savings fund. This will help you avoid temptation to overspend or undersave, and help you develop and build stronger habits of control over your money.

Open the Right Bank Accounts

Banks with limited physical infrastructure that provide online banking services are often able to operate without bank fees. And a well-organized budget works best when your money is divided into clear fee–free accounts. This alone will save you hundreds of dollars every year that can go toward your personal savings or paying off debts.

Setting up specific accounts will also help you quickly notice if you're allocating the appropriate percentage or amounts needed, based on your personal situation.

Here's the bank accounts setup you need:

1. Bank A:
    - Two transaction accounts with ATM access.
    - Two high interest savings accounts without ATM access.
2. Bank B.
    - One single bank account that earns high interest, with online access but no ATM access.

Coming up, we'll look at exactly how to allocate your specific budget into each of these accounts

Your Long-Term Goal: Financial Security

Don't overcomplicate it. Your ultimate goal is to be financially secure. That could mean retiring comfortably, buying a home, or achieving financial independence. Every part of your budget should support your long-term vision. And although your plan will be unique, based on where you start and exactly where you want to end up, to make this vision a reality, it's essential to keep your financial strategy straightforward and focused. Every element of your budget should align with this vision and support your long-term aspirations.

Strategies for Success

- Set realistic expectations.

    When starting a budget, it's easy to be overly ambitious, but that often leads to frustration. Give yourself some breathing room by setting realistic targets, especially for splurges. A sustainable budget allows for fun, so you're less likely to abandon it.

- Automate payments and savings allocations.

    One of the easiest ways to stick to your budget is by automating everything, from bills to savings contributions.

    Automating your finances is like putting your budget on autopilot. It makes your life simple and easy when it comes to managing your money.

- Make Adjustments.

    Budgets aren't meant to be rigid but to adapt as your life situation changes. Schedule a monthly check-in to review your progress. Celebrate your wins, and make adjustments. Notice if one of your accounts always seems to be running out of money or when another seems to have money left over at the end of the month. At this monthly

CHAPTER 4

check-in, always ask yourself, *What can I start, stop, or continue to do, to achieve my goals?*

And when you get a pay increase, decide exactly how much will go toward savings and how much to pay off your debts. You may consider recalculating your overall percentages, or my preferred option, direct an increased amount of money as you choose. If you want to get ahead quicker with your finances, keep your living expenses at the same amount, and avoid the salary creep. However, if your expenses do change, you will need to update your budget accordingly. The goal here is progress, not perfection.

With your budget firmly in place and understanding exactly where your money goes, you're now ready to handle the unexpected. In the next chapter, we'll explore how to build an emergency disaster fund to protect yourself from life's little surprises. Let's make saving for the unexpected easier and stress-free.

WEEK 4
SMALL STEPS TO THE FUTURE ABUNDANT YOU

- Calculate your current budget using the 60/20/10/10 DEAL method.
- Select two banks that offer fee-free banking.
  - ✓ In one bank, open four accounts: two transaction accounts with ATM access and two without.
  - ✓ In another bank open one high-interest account without ATM access as an emergency fund.

These five accounts will help you stay organized, automate your savings, control your spending, and stick to your long-term financial plan with ease.

CHAPTER 4

Dear Reader,

If you've made it this far, thank you. It means the world to me that you spent your time with this book, and I truly hope it's resonating with you in some way.

If you've found value in these pages, I have a small favor to ask: Would you consider leaving a review?

Your honest feedback helps more than you know. Reviews not only help other readers discover the book, but they also give me the encouragement (and insights!) to keep writing and improving.

It only takes a minute, but it makes a lasting impact.

Please leave your review on your store of choice or on Amazon by searching Money Power.

Scan the QR code below to learn more about me and my other books via my website.

Thank you again for being part of this journey with me.

With gratitude,

Janene

CHAPTER

DISASTER!
Build Your Safety Net

Do you have a plan for the unexpected?

Whether it's a sudden car breakdown, a medical bill, or a surprise expense, life will throw you curveballs. But when you have an emergency disaster fund, these events don't have to send you spiraling into debt. A solid financial safety net means you're prepared no matter what happens. Let's explore how to build and maintain your emergency fund, so you can focus on living your life with confidence.

CHAPTER 5

SECTION 1
THE ROLE OF AN EMERGENCY FUND

Emergencies aren't a matter of *if* but *when*. Car repairs, medical bills, sudden travel, or job loss can happen to anyone, often at the worst times. Without a plan, these expenses can lead to high-interest debt and financial stress.

Avoiding Emergency Debt

Credit cards and loans may seem like a lifeline during a crisis, but they come with high-interest rates that can trap you in debt. Having an emergency fund ensures you can handle surprises without borrowing, keeping you in control of your money.

So before focusing on larger financial goals, prioritize building an emergency fund. Aim to save at least three months' worth of living expenses as your starting point. This fund not only serves as a financial safety net but also provides significant psychological benefits.

Why Create an Emergency Fund?

- Peace of mind

  Having an emergency fund creates a sense of security and stability.

- Reduced stress and anxiety

  Financial stress is one of the leading causes of anxiety in modern life. Even minor financial setbacks can feel overwhelming. Establishing an emergency fund mitigates this stress, acting as a buffer, so you can manage unexpected expenses without derailing your financial plans or losing focus.

- Increased resilience

    An emergency fund enables you to bounce back more effectively from setbacks. When you face a financial challenge, having savings to draw upon can prevent you from resorting to high-interest loans or credit cards, which can lead to a cycle of debt.

- Better decision-making

    When your finances are secure, you're better positioned to make thoughtful, strategic decisions regarding your larger financial goals, such as saving for retirement or buying a home. Without the pressure of immediate financial concerns, you can approach these decisions with a clear mind and a longer-term perspective, which leads to more thoughtful investments that align with your values and aspirations.

- Build a savings habit

    Creating an emergency fund is an excellent way to cultivate a habit of saving, with a focus on financial responsibility and proactive planning. As you consistently contribute to this fund, you develop discipline and a greater understanding of budgeting that serves you well in all areas of your financial life. It's then easier to save for other goals, as the habit becomes ingrained.

- Enhancing financial confidence

    Finally, having an emergency fund boosts your financial confidence and empowers you to face financial challenges with the assurance that you have a plan in place. It permeates other aspects of your life, including a willingness to pursue new opportunities without fear of financial ruin.

In summary, prioritizing an emergency fund before tackling larger financial goals isn't just a practical step, it's a psychologically beneficial one.

CHAPTER 5

Financial Disaster: Michelle's story

When I was growing up, my older sister, Michelle, was my biggest source of encouragement and support. In my eyes, she could do anything. Whatever she did seemed effortless. She ran faster, always won at board games, and could draw and paint, all of which I always wanted to do. When we were older, Michelle came to me, because her washing machine had broken down. I was thankful I'd set up my own emergency fund, so I was able to help her without hesitation. After the new machine was delivered, I walked her through how to start saving, and set up her own accounts.

Two years later, Michelle's car broke down and needed a new transmission. She came to me once again, asking if I could help with the mechanic's bill, promising to pay me back. This time, instead of immediately offering my assistance, I asked her why she hadn't used the money from her own emergency fund I'd encouraged her to set up, and was disappointed to learn she hadn't created one.

Michelle had always been a carefree spirit, preferring not to worry about anything, until it actually happened. She lived with a go-with-the-flow attitude, trusting that the Universe would work things out when the time came. She never thought it necessary to prepare for unexpected expenses, instead handling situations as they arose, always figuring it out in the moment. Unfortunately, this led her into two stressful situations that could have easily been avoided.

What I learned from this experience is that knowing what to do isn't enough. You have to take action, and break the old habits that no longer align with your goals, in order to achieve different results. The habit of reacting to situations rather than preparing for them, is more common than most people realize. Don't let that be you. If you want to change your financial future, start planning and preparing today, rather than reacting when things go wrong.

DISASTER!

SECTION 2
CREATING YOUR SAFETY NET

Step 1: Create a $2,000 emergency disaster fund.

Don't let the idea of an emergency fund overwhelm you. Here are a few ways to quickly achieve a two-thousand-dollar goal:

- Sell unused items.

  Go through your belongings, and sell items you no longer need, such as clothing, electronics, furniture, or collectibles, through online marketplaces or garage sales.

- Do odd jobs

  There's babysitting, dog walking/sitting, or mowing lawns.

- Do freelance or gig work.

  Leverage your skills by taking on freelance work or gig jobs, such as graphic design, writing, or driving for rideshare services. Use online platforms like Upwork or Fivver.

- Get a part-time job.

  Consider picking up a part-time job or seasonal work to earn extra income, especially during busy times like the holidays or the summer months.

    - ✓ Participate in online surveys

      Sign up for websites that pay you to take surveys or participate in market research. While this won't yield a lot, it can add up.

    - ✓ Rent out a room or property

      If you have extra space in your home, consider renting it out on platforms like Airbnb or finding a long-term roommate.

- ✓ Use cash-back and rewards programs

    Utilize cash-back apps and credit card rewards to earn money on everyday purchases.

- ✓ Look for temporary work

    Contract positions can provide immediate income without a long-term commitment.

- ✓ Return unused purchases

    If you have items you've never used, consider returning them to the store for a refund.

Deposit the accumulated money into your Bank B account, the one with the high-interest savings and no ATM access. Now you have something to fall back on immediately, even before you reach your larger savings target.

Once you hit your two-thousand-dollar milestone, remember to celebrate with one of your small wins.

Step 2: Calculate the larger savings target

Next, it's time to focus on your larger goal, that being three months of essential fixed living expenses. These include rent or mortgage, groceries, utilities, and insurance payments. From the 60/20/10/10 rule, you will have calculated sixty percent of your total take-home pay. Multiply that sixty percent figure times three. This will give you your next target goal, and give you a full three months without financial panic.

- ▸ Set up an automatic transfer into your bank B account, so there's no temptation to dip into it.

Step 3: Increase your fund

At this point, increase your emergency fund to cover six months or more of your fixed expenses. I would just suggest that you circle back to this step after the other accounts are all set up and operating to a level you're happy with.

SECTION 3
MAINTAINING YOUR FUND

➤ When It's Okay to Use the Disaster Fund

Acceptable uses for your emergency fund include the following:

- ✓ Medical emergencies not covered by insurance.
- ✓ Urgent car repairs
- ✓ Emergency home maintenance or repairs, like plumbing leaks or roof damage.
- ✓ Transition period following job loss.
- ✓ Last-minute travel expenses for family emergencies, such as a funeral or urgent situation.
- ✓ Veterinary bills for sudden illnesses or accidents.
- ✓ Expenses incurred due to a natural disaster like hurricanes and earthquakes.
- ✓ Costs associated with resolving identity theft, including legal fees and credit monitoring services.
- ✓ Unforeseen legal expenses, such as hiring a lawyer for a sudden court case or dispute.
- ✓ Sudden bills that arise, such as a utility bill spike or property tax assessment.
- ✓ Financial support for family members during crises, such as illness or loss of income.

Avoid dipping into your fund for non-emergencies, like holidays or impulse purchases. Protect your safety net. You'll thank yourself later.

CHAPTER 5

➢ Replenishing

If you do need to use your emergency fund, make replenishing it your top priority. Adjust your budget temporarily to direct extra funds toward rebuilding it back up.

➢ Automate Contributions

Set up an automatic transfer from your number one income account to your emergency disaster fund each month. Initially, this is twenty percent of your take-home income. Even small regular contributions add up over time and require no extra effort.

SECTION 4
INSURANCE FOR UNEXPECTED EVENTS

An emergency fund alone can't cover everything, and insurance is your second line of defense. The right insurance protects you from major financial setbacks. Did you know that over one-hundred-thousand Australians suffer work-related injuries each year? Without insurance, these events can wipe out your savings.

Types of Insurance to Consider

- Life insurance

    Protects your family financially if you pass away.

- Income protection insurance

    Provides a portion of your salary if you're unable to work due to illness or injury.

- Home and contents insurance

    Covers damage to your property and belongings from accidents or natural disasters.

- Total and permanent disability (TPD) insurance

    Provides a lump sum if you're permanently unable to work.

- Car insurance

    Protects you from accidental damage, severe weather, fire, or theft.

CHAPTER 5

How to Set Up Insurance

Talk to a financial advisor or insurance broker to find the policies that fit your needs. When choosing providers, look for transparent policies with good customer reviews. Avoid overpaying by comparing coverage and fees. Many people are overinsured without realizing it.

Note: Avoid using those companies that compare all your brokers for you. First, they don't have every single broker on their books, and second, they're more expensive.

Make Your Money Work for You

With your emergency disaster fund in place and insurance as your backup, you're ready to move from defense to offense. It's time to start building wealth through allocation and investing. In the next chapter, we'll explore how to allocate your money to work for you, so you can enjoy financial freedom and long-term security. Let's dive into the exciting world of investing.

WEEK 5
SMALL STEPS TO THE FUTURE ABUNDANT YOU

- Build your initial disaster fund.

    Focus on creating or saving your first two thousand as quickly as possible. Once saved, deposit it into your high-interest savings account with bank B.

- Set your first short-term goal.

    Calculate the total amount needed to cover three months of your essential fixed living expenses. As you continue building toward this goal, deposit the funds into your bank B account. Increase this amount only after all other accounts are well funded.

- Set up insurance.

    Find a local financial broker who can assist you in establishing the necessary insurance coverage to protect you against unforeseen circumstances.

CHAPTER

ALLOCATE
If you don't see the money, you won't miss it.

The easiest way to save and build wealth isn't by relying on willpower. It's by automating your finances. When your savings and investments are deducted automatically, there's no need to decide whether to save each month. Paying yourself first means directing money toward your goals the moment it arrives. Let's explore how automation gives you the freedom to enjoy today, and a solid foundation for long-term security.

CHAPTER 6

SECTION 1

WHY AUTOMATION WORKS

Did you know that as individuals we make between thirty-three thousand and thirty-five thousand total conscious decisions every day? This includes what time we wake up, if we snooze the alarm, what we eat, what we wear, what we say, and how we say it. So, when decisions are required about whether you want to save or spend, you risk falling into decision fatigue, which is the exhaustion from making too many small choices. Automating your savings eliminates this mental drain. Once your system is in place, the savings process runs quietly in the background, leaving you free to focus on other things that matter to you!

Direct Deposits and Automated Transfers

By setting up direct deposits from your paycheck or automated transfers from your transaction account to your savings or investment accounts, you make sure your money goes exactly where you want it before you have a chance to spend it.

You're effectively prioritizing saving and investing over impulsive purchases. This "pay yourself first" approach encourages discipline and a habit of saving that can lead to greater financial security over time.

By treating savings as a nonnegotiable expense, you create a buffer against lifestyle inflation and unforeseen expenses, so your savings grow consistently. This can be particularly beneficial for building up your emergency disaster fund, saving for your retirement, or funding specific financial goals.

Automation also means you won't have to remember to manually move money each month, reducing the likelihood of forgetting or postponing savings. Knowing that you're actively working toward your financial goals without the stress of daily financial decisions provides peace of mind and sets the foundational habit for long-term success.

ALLOCATE

How to Optimize the Accounts

Step 1: Direct all your income into the first income account.

Step 2: Allocate your money using the 60/20/10/10 rule.

> Sixty percent remains in the number one income account and is designated for all your *everyday expenses*.

> Twenty percent is directed toward building your emergency *disaster* fund, until it reaches an amount that covers three months of your fixed living expenses. The funds will then be redirected toward *debt* repayment, including credit cards and loans.

> Ten percent is allocated to future savings for goals you *aspire* to; like a vacation or car, and eventually, buying a home or investment property.

> Ten percent is dedicated to short-term *luxuries* that bring you joy.

CHAPTER 6

Here's a diagram that visually represents the income split based on the provided categories. Each section of the pie chart indicates the percentage allocated to different areas, including everyday expenses, disaster and debt repayment funds, short and long term savings and also money for luxuries and fun.

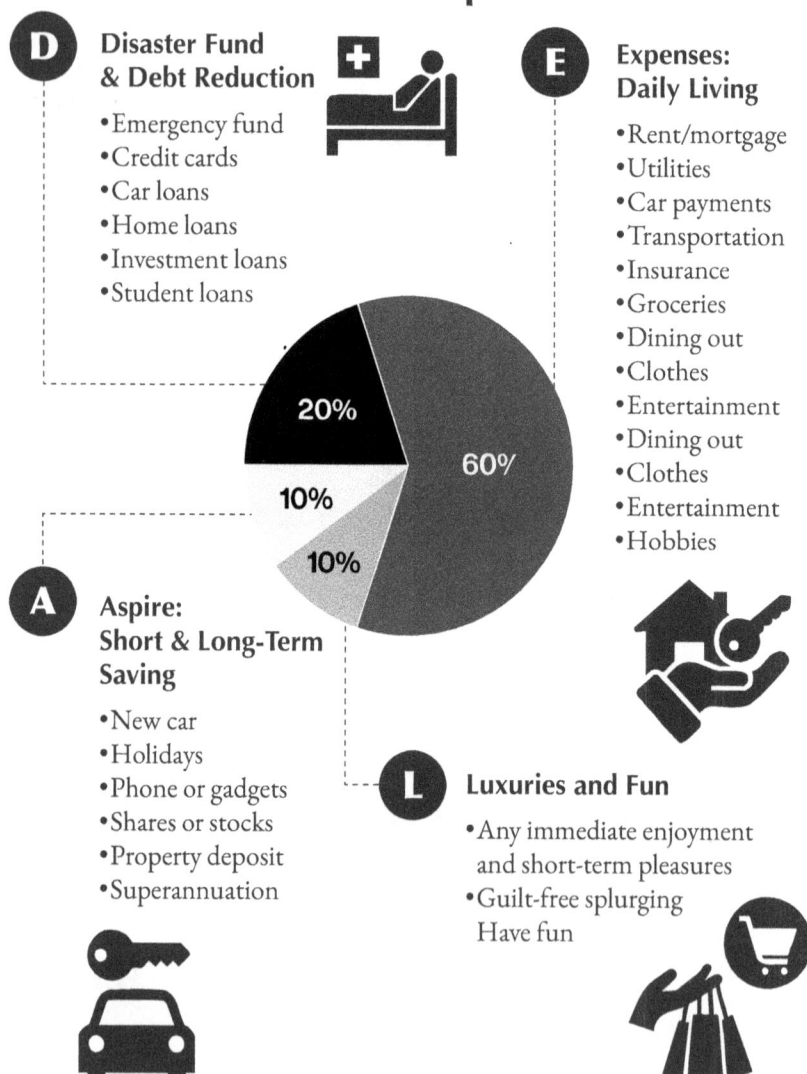

Here's the DEAL Income Split

D — Disaster Fund & Debt Reduction
- Emergency fund
- Credit cards
- Car loans
- Home loans
- Investment loans
- Student loans

E — Expenses: Daily Living
- Rent/mortgage
- Utilities
- Car payments
- Transportation
- Insurance
- Groceries
- Dining out
- Clothes
- Entertainment
- Dining out
- Clothes
- Entertainment
- Hobbies

20%
60%
10%
10%

A — Aspire: Short & Long-Term Saving
- New car
- Holidays
- Phone or gadgets
- Shares or stocks
- Property deposit
- Superannuation

L — Luxuries and Fun
- Any immediate enjoyment and short-term pleasures
- Guilt-free splurging Have fun

ALLOCATE

How to Save Without Noticing: Rachel's Story

Rachel, a high school teacher, decided to automate two-hundred dollars from each paycheck into a high-interest savings account. Because the transfer happened automatically on payday, she barely noticed the missing amount. A year later, she was delighted to find that she'd saved over $10,000 -without even feeling like she was cutting back.

In the end, her biggest decision was whether to put her efforts into updating her car or going on holiday.

CHAPTER 6

SECTION 2
SETTING UP AUTOMATION

Most banks offer automated transfer options within their online services or apps. Set up recurring transfers to move a portion of your income to savings and investment accounts. You can also schedule bill and debt repayments to stay on track without effort.

To effectively automate your finances, begin by reviewing all of your regular fixed expenses, including monthly bills and less frequent costs like annual car registration or insurance. Once you have an overview, set up automated transfers through your bank's online services or mobile app. These all come from the sixty percent that remains sitting in your number one bank account.

For quarterly utility bills, set up direct debits or recurring monthly payments. Divide your typical quarterly bill by three to determine the monthly payment needed to cover it fully when it comes due, and transfer this amount directly to the utility company each month. While there may be small variations, you'll have the majority of the bill paid off in advance.

For less frequent larger annual expenses like your car registration or insurance, you can leave funds in your main account to gradually accumulate the necessary amount each month. As the months pass, you'll see the balance steadily growing. This method simplifies financial management and helps you stay on top of both routine and occasional financial obligations.

Employer Savings Programs

If you're in Australia, superannuation is a powerful automated savings tool for retirement. However, not all funds are created equal. Many charge high fees that can eat away at your balance over time. You must look for ultra-low-fee super funds.

This diagram illustrates the different superannuation funds, the first with a low-fee structure and the second with a higher fee structure over forty years.

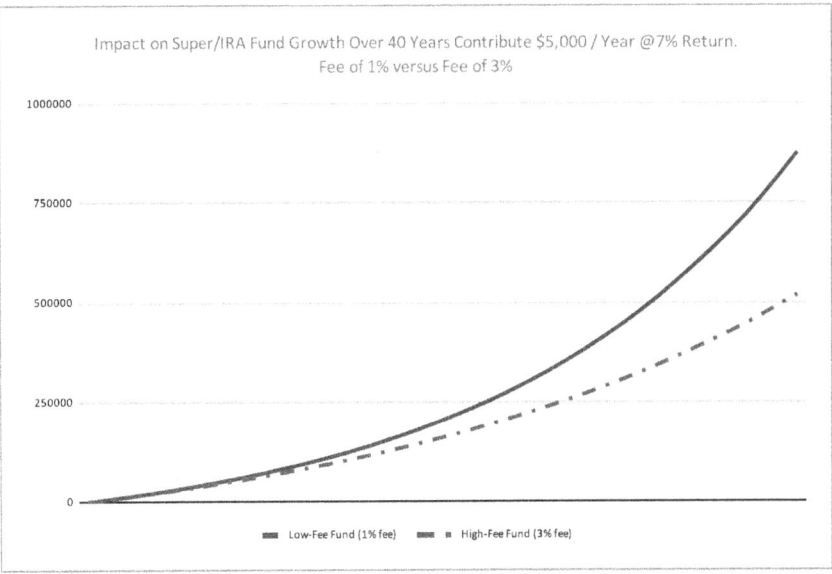

The chart above illustrates the growth of superannuation amounts over a forty-year timeline, comparing a low-fee fund to a higher-fee fund. Each has an annual contribution of five thousand dollars, and earning an average seven percent annual return.

In forty years' time, you would have $519,098 in the high-fee fund, while the low-fee fund would have accumulated $874,753. That's a massive difference of over $350k, for making one small informed decision.

As you can see, the lower fees significantly enhance the total amount accumulated over time. You'll also notice the detailed data in the accompanying table.

CHAPTER 6

Year	Annual Contribution	Low-Fee Fund (1% fee)	High-Fee Fund (3% fee)	Difference (Low - High)
0	$ 5,000	0	0	0
1	$ 5,000	$ 5,300	$ 5,200	$ 100
2	$ 5,000	$ 10,918	$ 10,608	$ 310
3	$ 5,000	$ 16,873	$ 16,232	$ 641
4	$ 5,000	$ 23,185	$ 22,082	$ 1,104
5	$ 5,000	$ 29,877	$ 28,165	$ 1,712
6	$ 5,000	$ 36,969	$ 34,491	$ 2,478
7	$ 5,000	$ 44,487	$ 41,071	$ 3,416
8	$ 5,000	$ 52,457	$ 47,914	$ 4,543
9	$ 5,000	$ 60,904	$ 55,031	$ 5,873
10	$ 5,000	$ 69,858	$ 62,432	$ 7,426
11	$ 5,000	$ 79,350	$ 70,129	$ 9,221
12	$ 5,000	$ 89,411	$ 78,134	$ 11,276
13	$ 5,000	$ 100,075	$ 86,460	$ 13,616
14	$ 5,000	$ 111,380	$ 95,118	$ 16,262
15	$ 5,000	$ 123,363	$ 104,123	$ 19,240
16	$ 5,000	$ 136,064	$ 113,488	$ 22,577
17	$ 5,000	$ 149,528	$ 123,227	$ 26,301
18	$ 5,000	$ 163,800	$ 133,356	$ 30,444
19	$ 5,000	$ 178,928	$ 143,890	$ 35,038
20	$ 5,000	$ 194,964	$ 154,846	$ 40,118
21	$ 5,000	$ 211,961	$ 166,240	$ 45,722
22	$ 5,000	$ 229,979	$ 178,089	$ 51,890
23	$ 5,000	$ 249,078	$ 190,413	$ 58,665
24	$ 5,000	$ 269,323	$ 203,230	$ 66,093
25	$ 5,000	$ 290,782	$ 216,559	$ 74,223
26	$ 5,000	$ 313,529	$ 230,421	$ 83,108
27	$ 5,000	$ 337,641	$ 244,838	$ 92,803
28	$ 5,000	$ 363,199	$ 259,831	$ 103,368
29	$ 5,000	$ 390,291	$ 275,425	$ 114,866
30	$ 5,000	$ 419,008	$ 291,642	$ 127,367
31	$ 5,000	$ 449,449	$ 308,507	$ 140,942
32	$ 5,000	$ 481,716	$ 326,048	$ 155,668
33	$ 5,000	$ 515,919	$ 344,290	$ 171,629
34	$ 5,000	$ 552,174	$ 363,261	$ 188,913
35	$ 5,000	$ 590,604	$ 382,992	$ 207,613
36	$ 5,000	$ 631,341	$ 403,511	$ 227,829
37	$ 5,000	$ 674,521	$ 424,852	$ 249,669
38	$ 5,000	$ 720,292	$ 447,046	$ 273,247
39	$ 5,000	$ 768,810	$ 470,128	$ 298,682
40	$ 5,000	$ 820,238	$ 494,133	$ 326,106
41	$ 5,000	$ 874,753	$ 519,098	$ 355,655

ALLOCATE

Investment and Round-Up Apps

Apps like Raiz and Spaceship in Australia offer innovative ways to invest small amounts automatically, making it accessible for individuals who want to start building wealth with minimal effort. With these platforms, you can set up regular contributions or use features like round-ups, where purchases made with your linked bank card are rounded up to the nearest dollar, and the difference is automatically invested. For example, if you buy a coffee for $3.60, the app rounds it up to four dollars and saves the extra forty cents, so you can passively grow your investments over time.

Both apps offer diversified portfolios tailored to different risk levels, eliminating the need for you to research or manage individual stocks.

CHAPTER 6

SECTION 3
MAINTAINING MOMENTUM: ADJUSTING AUTOMATION

Increase Savings

When your income rises, it can be tempting to upgrade your lifestyle by splurging on new purchases, a phenomenon known as lifestyle inflation. However, this is also a prime opportunity to increase your automated savings.

Allocating a portion of your extra income, such as from raises or bonuses, allows you to enjoy a portion of your extra earnings guilt-free while putting the rest to work for your long-term goals. Over time, consistently redirecting a portion of increased income can lead to significant wealth accumulation, providing a cushion for emergencies, faster debt repayment, or greater financial independence, all while maintaining a balanced lifestyle.

Celebrate Milestones

Celebrating savings milestones invigorates motivation and momentum. Every time you achieve a significant goal, such as paying off a credit card or clearing a loan balance, it's important to acknowledge your progress, as it creates a sense of accomplishment, making it more likely you'll stay committed to your financial goals. Remember that list of small, medium, and larger rewards you created earlier? This is the perfect time to put it to use. Choose a reward that aligns with the size of your achievement.

You tap into the psychology of reward-based motivation, as our brains are wired to seek pleasure and avoid pain, so celebrating wins releases dopamine, the feel-good hormone, which reinforces the behavior that led to the achievement. By giving yourself planned, meaningful rewards, you create positive associations with saving and financial discipline, making it more enjoyable and sustainable over the long term. This approach transforms your financial journey from being purely about sacrifice to a more balanced and rewarding experience, keeping you excited and engaged in reaching the next milestone.

Automate Savings

Set up automated transfers from your primary income account into your separate high-interest-earning account. Most people report that watching their progress grow keeps them motivated and on track without the stress of doing everything manually.

Protect Your Wealth

Saving and investing on autopilot is a powerful tool for building wealth, but it's only one part of the equation. To truly secure your financial future, you must manage debt effectively, so you have total control over your finances and can make your money work harder for you. In the next chapter, we'll dive into strategies to ensure debt doesn't derail your progress, so you can keep moving toward financial freedom. Let's take control of debt, so you stay on track.

CHAPTER 6

WEEK 6
SMALL STEPS TO THE FUTURE ABUNDANT YOU

➢ Notify your employer

Submit a written notice to your employer with the details of your new superannuation/IRA account, so all future contributions are directed to the low-fee fund you've chosen. This simple step helps you maximize your retirement savings by avoiding unnecessary fees.

➢ Set up automated transfers from your number one income account

Automate your financial system by creating a direct transfer the day after payday from your primary income account with ATM access. Keep sixty percent of your pay in this account for essential living **EXPENSES,** and distribute the rest across your other accounts: twenty percent for **DEBT** repayment, ten percent to splurge on **LUXURIES,** and ten percent for savings goals you **ASPIRE** too. This helps you stay in control of your finances.

➢ Automate debt payments

Set up automated payments toward your highest-priority debt. Whenever possible, increase your payments with bonuses and tax refunds, to reach your debt-free milestones faster.

PART C

WHERE DO YOU WANT TO BE?

CHAPTER

NAVIGATE DEBT AS A TOOL

Not all debt is bad, but knowing the difference could save you.

Debt can feel overwhelming, but it doesn't have to be. When managed wisely, it can be a powerful tool for building wealth and creating opportunities. The key is knowing the difference between good debt that helps you grow financially, and bad debt that ultimately drains your financial resources. In this chapter, we'll look at the Return on Investment method of strategic debt management and understand how to use credit responsibly and strategically.

CHAPTER 7

RULE 1
BE RESPONSIBLE WITH CREDIT

Understanding the difference between good and bad debt is crucial to making responsible financial decisions. Good debt is generally seen as an investment that has the potential to grow in value or generate long-term income. In the finance world, this is referred to as a return on investment or ROI. Bad debt, on the other hand, typically carries high interest rates, often leading to financial stress. Here are some examples of good debt:

> Mortgage

   A mortgage is often considered good debt, because it can help you build wealth over time. Each payment you make goes toward building equity, which is the portion of your house that you truly own.

   Over time, as you pay down your mortgage, and your home's value appreciates, your equity grows. This can act as a form of forced savings, and you may eventually be able to tap into this equity to finance other goals, such as home improvements, education, or even starting a business.

> Student loans

   Education is often considered a powerful investment in your future earning potential and career development. While taking on student loans can initially feel burdensome, a college degree or specialized training can significantly increase lifetime earnings and open doors to better job opportunities, career advancement, and benefits.

   For example, studies consistently show that people with higher levels of education tend to earn more over their careers compared to those without a degree. The key is to borrow wisely, seek scholarships, and ensure the degree pursued aligns with strong job market demand.

   However, don't rush to pay them off early if the interest rates are low, especially in countries like Australia, where repayment thresholds align with your income. You'll often get more value by investing spare cash elsewhere, like in shares or your superannuation, which could yield higher returns.

- Business loans

  Borrowing money to start or expand a business can lead to substantial financial returns and wealth creation over time. Business loans provide the capital needed for new equipment, hiring staff, expanding operations, or developing new products.

  While there's always some risk involved, a well-planned business venture can generate steady income and build equity. Entrepreneurs who leverage business loans strategically often find that their investments yield far greater returns than the interest paid on the loans themselves.

- Home equity loans

  Home equity loans allow homeowners to borrow against the value of their homes, providing funds for various purposes, such as improvements or renovations. By using this loan for strategic upgrades, like a kitchen remodel or an additional bedroom, you can increase your property's market value and improve your living conditions. This, in turn, can lead to higher resale value and greater equity.

  The interest on these loans may also be tax-deductible, so there's an additional financial advantage. A word of caution: The renovation must be a strategic one, which means you renovate for profit, not simply for what's referred to as "keeping up with the Joneses," where you renovate because the neighbors did.

- Investment loans

  Borrowing money to invest in appreciating assets like stocks, bonds, or real estate can be a form of good debt when done strategically. Investment loans amplify your potential gains by giving you access to larger capital than you have available.

  For example, taking out a mortgage to purchase a rental property could generate passive income, while a carefully leveraged stock portfolio may offer high returns over time. However, it's essential to understand and manage the risks involved. Market fluctuations can impact returns, so as a borrower, you must conduct thorough

CHAPTER 7

research, diversify investments, and know you can manage payments, even in downturns.

Here are some examples of what's considered bad debt. These rarely provide any ROI and often create financial stress in the long run:

- Credit card debt

   Credit card debt is a common example of bad debt, due to its typically high interest rates, which can range from fifteen to thirty percent or more. When balances are carried from month to month, interest charges can quickly accumulate, making it challenging to pay off the principal amount.

   Unlike investments in appreciating assets, credit card purchases often provide no long-term value. Once the item is consumed or used, you're still left with the debt. Relying heavily on credit cards can lead to a cycle of debt that's difficult to escape, which reduces your financial stability and future savings potential. Unlike a mortgage, credit card interest isn't tax-deductible, and it doesn't increase your net worth.

- Payday loans

   Payday loans are short-term, high-interest loans designed to provide quick cash, often targeting people in urgent need of money. The downside is their extremely high annual percentage rates (APR), which can exceed four-hundred percent.

   They often require full repayment within a short period, usually by the borrower's next paycheck. And if they can't repay on time, they may be forced to roll over the loan, incurring additional fees and creating a cycle of debt.

- Luxury auto loans

   Auto loans for luxury vehicles often represent bad debt, because cars rapidly depreciate in value as soon as they're driven off the lot. Luxury models typically come with higher price tags, interest rates, insurance costs, and maintenance expenses, without providing any financial return.

Unlike a home or an investment, vehicles don't build equity and lose value over time. Investing heavily in a depreciating asset can hinder long-term financial goals and leave you with high monthly payments for a product that loses value with every mile driven.

> Consumer loans

Taking out loans to purchase nonessential items, such as electronics or to finance vacations, can lead to debt that offers no financial return and depreciates rapidly.

Electronics often become outdated quickly, and borrowing to fund a vacation means paying high interest on something that offers no lasting financial value. While these items may provide short-term enjoyment, the debt accrued can linger long after the initial excitement wears off.

> Retail store cards

Retail store cards often entice consumers with promotions like discounts on initial purchases, exclusive sales, or loyalty rewards. However, these cards typically come with high-interest rates, often much higher than standard credit cards.

Additionally, they encourage spending beyond your means by promoting impulse purchases and store-specific rewards. When balances aren't paid in full each month, interest charges quickly accumulate, negating any initial savings.

Case Study: A Tale of Two Spenders

When Jenna returned from her dream vacation in Europe, she was filled with stories to tell and photos to share, but there was one unwelcome souvenir: the twelve-thousand-dollar credit card bill. The trip had been spontaneous, sparked by a social media post showing a friend's Paris adventures, and she'd financed the entire vacation on her credit card. At first, Jenna justified the splurge, telling herself the three weeks of fun and excitement were worth it. But as the months passed, and interest continued to build, the thrill of the trip faded. Each time she made a minimum payment, the debt hardly budged. What was once a dream vacation had become a heavy financial burden, lingering long after the tan faded.

CHAPTER 7

In contrast, Jenna's friend Alex took a different approach. He decided to buy a modest home in the suburbs, taking on a $600,000 mortgage and putting down twenty percent of his savings. It wasn't easy, and there were months when he had to tighten his belt. But with each mortgage payment, Alex built equity in his home.

Over time, his neighborhood became increasingly desirable, and the value of his home rose by $100,000. When Alex needed funds to start his small business, he was able to refinance by tapping into his home equity.

While Jenna's debt became a lasting burden, Alex's debt served as a foundation for growth and security.

RULE 2
OPTIMIZE DEBT-REPAYMENT STRATEGIES

Paying off existing debt as quickly as possible is a vital step in achieving financial health and stability. When you carry high-interest debt, like credit cards or personal loans, interest compounds over time, increasing the total amount you owe and making it more difficult to get ahead financially.

Becoming debt-free reduces stress and anxiety associated with financial burdens, improves your credit score, and increases your ability to access better loan terms in the future. It also gives you greater flexibility in your budget to make decisions that align with your financial aspirations without the constant drain of monthly debt payments. The sooner you pay down debt, the more financial freedom and security you can enjoy. In terms of a repayment solution, you can choose from these two options:

- Snowball Method

    The snowball method helps you build motivation by paying off the smallest debts first, regardless of interest rates. Every time you clear a debt, you gain a psychological win, which keeps you motivated to continue. This method works great if you feel overwhelmed by debt and need quick wins to stay on track.

    Remember that snapshot list of debts/loans you made? You're now going to use this to prioritize which debt to focus on paying off first. And if two loan amounts are similar, choose the one that has the higher interest rate.

    Once the first card or loan is paid off, move on to the next smallest on your list. This small habit builds momentum and creates some great motivation. And it feels so good to watch your cards and loans get paid out!

CHAPTER 7

> Avalanche Method

The avalanche method focuses on paying off the highest-interest debts first. Although it may take longer to see the first win, you'll save more money over time by reducing the amount of interest you pay. You would use the avalanche method if your top priority is minimizing long-term costs.

While both of these repayment methods are effective for reducing your debt in the long term, it just seems better to create the habit of small psychological wins early.

Once your high-interest credit cards and personal loans are paid off, the extra money you've freed up can be directed toward a range of productive and financially empowering goals. Remember the DEAL. Your unique situation will determine which goals you ASPIRE to, aligning with your personal risk tolerance and individual values. Here are some options for you to consider:

> Build or Strengthen Your 'Disaster' Fund

Save three to six months' worth of living expenses in an emergency fund, as this provides financial security in case of expensive unexpected events, such as job loss or medical emergencies. With your debt payments out of the way, this fund builds faster.

> Contribute to Retirement Accounts

Maximize contributions to retirement accounts like a 401(k), Superannuation/IRA, or other retirement savings plans, as the earlier you start contributing, the more time your money has to grow through compound interest.

If your employer offers a Super/401(k) match, aim to contribute enough to take full advantage of it. Options like a Traditional or Roth IRA offer tax benefits that can further boost your savings, while contributing to a 401(k) plan, especially with matching contributions, is often a smart choice for securing your financial future.

> Invest in Assets or Investment Accounts

Grow your wealth over time through investments, as it offers the potential for higher returns compared to savings accounts or cash.

Whether you choose stocks, bonds, or real estate, investments help secure your financial future. Options like exchange traded funds (ETFs) or index funds provide low-cost, diversified investment strategies, while real estate can be a smart way to build for your home while creating capital growth.

➤ Pay Down Other Debts

Tackle any remaining debt, such as mortgages or student loans. To do this efficiently, you can use the snowball or avalanche method.

➤ Save for Large Future Purchases

Start saving for a down payment on a home, car, or other significant purchase. This can lower monthly payments, and reduce interest costs. To stay organized and focused, consider opening a separate savings account specifically for this large goal, which will allow you to track your progress, and keep the money separate from your regular spending.

➤ Improve Your Employability

Invest in personal development and education to increase your earning potential. Taking financial literacy courses or working with a financial advisor can also help you make smarter investments.

➤ Make Home Improvements or Repairs

This goal is to increase the value of your home, or make it more comfortable in order to raise its value, and save money on future repairs. Options include upgrading appliances, renovating rooms, or repairing structural issues, as well as investing in energy-efficient improvements that can reduce future utility bills.

➤ Travel or Go on Adventures

Use extra money for personal enrichment or experiences, as life isn't solely about financial stability but also enjoying the present and enriching your experiences.

CHAPTER 7

> Make Charitable Contributions

Donate to causes that matter to you and positively impact the lives of others. Charitable donations also offer tax deductions if you itemize them.

> Build or Expand Your Business

Use the additional funds to start or grow your own business, as the extra money can be an investment in launching a side hustle or expanding an existing business if you have entrepreneurial ambitions. You can use the funds to buy necessary tools, pay for marketing, or hire help to get the business off the ground, and set it up for success.

After paying off your credit cards and personal loans, the additional money can help you invest in your future, and build a legacy for generations to come. The key is to balance short-term enjoyment with long-term financial goals, and continue making smart, well-informed decisions with your money.

Of all of the potential goals to aspire to, my personal focus instilled into me by my mother, was home ownership, and I guess that's often been the Aussie way! It's a great savings plan and is often considered a roadmap to building wealth and financial security. As property values in many parts of Australia tend to rise over time, owning a home allows you to build equity, which is essentially a forced savings plan.

Instead of paying rent, which contributes to someone else's wealth, mortgage payments go toward owning a tangible asset that can appreciate in value.

The Importance of Homeownership

Owning your own home provides a permanent place of residence, offering emotional security, and a sense of belonging. It also lays the foundation for future generations by creating a legacy of financial stability, breaking cycles of renting and uncertainty. Homeownership promotes independence, self-sufficiency, and self-worth. Moreover, with each mortgage payment, you reinforce the habit of good investing, as you build equity, unlike renting, which offers no return on your payments.

Let's look at what to consider when saving the 'traditional' way.

Saving for Your First Home in Twenty Months

Determine Your Desired Home

- Research Local Housing Markets

  Begin by researching housing prices in the area where you'd like to live. This will help you set a realistic price range based on your savings and income. Understand the general cost of homes, including factors like the location and condition of the property. Don't forget to factor in the price of utilities, property taxes, and home insurance.

- Define Your Needs and Wants

  Distinguish between needs and wants. For example, while a backyard may be a must-have, a swimming pool may be a luxury. This helps streamline your search and focuses your savings efforts.

- Be Realistic

  While it's important to dream, setting a realistic price range allows you to save effectively and avoid getting discouraged later. It also means you don't stretch your finances too thin when the time comes to buy. If the prices are higher than you're able to pay, find a location farther out from the town centers, go more outer suburbs, or even consider going rural.

Set Your Target Timeline

- Establish a Clear Goal

  Decide when you want to buy your home. Having a concrete timeline allows you to break down the savings process into manageable steps, and adjust when necessary.

- Set a Realistic Timeframe

  Consider your current savings, income and lifestyle when setting your target. Be realistic about how much you can save each month, and the potential for income increases or side jobs. If your timeline is too short, you may feel overwhelmed, but if it's too long, you may lose motivation.

CHAPTER 7

Review Your Current Finances

➢ Assess Income, Expenses, and Debts

Go back, and take a hard and close look at your finances. What is your monthly income? How can this be increased? What are your essential expenses? How can you reduce these further, even if only for a short time? What can you stop, start, or continue doing to help you achieve this goal faster? Reassessing your financial standing with this goal in mind helps determine how much you can save each month, and where you need to cut back.

➢ Establish Your Savings Rate

Based on your financial assessment, calculate how much you can comfortably save each month. Consistency is key, so try to regularly put aside a set amount.

➢ Redirect Savings

Once you've identified areas to cut back, redirect those funds into your home savings account. Even if it's only a small amount initially, this discipline will accumulate over time, and help you stay on track to reach your goal.

Understand the Costs of Homeownership

➢ Down Payment/ Deposit

Typically, a down payment is ten-twenty percent of the home's price. For example, if the home costs three-hundred-thousand, a twenty percent down payment would be sixty-thousand dollars. While there are some low down-payment options, saving for a larger down payment can help reduce your monthly mortgage and avoid private mortgage insurance (PMI), or what we call Lenders Mortgage Insurance (LMI) in Australia.

➢ Closing Costs

These include a variety of fees, such as title insurance, home inspections, and appraisal fees, typically adding up to two-five percent of the home price. It's important to budget for these additional expenses when planning for your purchase.

> Ongoing Costs

   Beyond the down payment and closing costs, homeownership comes with ongoing expenses, including mortgage payments, property taxes, insurance, utilities, and maintenance. Be sure to account for these ongoing financial commitments.

Additional Strategies to Boost Your Savings

Income Increases

> Side Hustles and Passive Income

   Consider finding a part-time job, freelancing, or investing in skills that allow you to earn extra income. Side hustles like tutoring, dog-walking, or creating content, can provide a steady influx of cash that goes directly into your home savings.

> Tax Refunds or Bonuses

   If you receive a tax refund, work bonus, or other financial windfalls, use these unexpected funds to give your savings a significant boost.

Down Payment Assistance Programs

> Government Programs

   Research state or local home loan or deposit assistance programs available for first-time homebuyers. Many regions offer grants, low-interest loans, or deferred loans to help with the upfront cost of buying a home. These programs can help you reduce the amount you need to save for your down payment.

> Mortgage Broker

   A mortgage broker specializing in first-time homebuyers can guide you through the options available, including assistance programs, and help you understand your eligibility offering advice on financing options that best suit your financial situation.

CHAPTER 7

Negotiating a lower mortgage interest rate

When your home loans are established, you'll want to optimize your current loans. Negotiating a lower interest rate on your mortgage loan can provide significant financial benefits.

A reduced interest rate decreases the total cost of your loan, potentially saving you thousands of dollars over the life of the mortgage. It also lowers your monthly payments, freeing up cash for other financial goals, like home improvements. You may even be able to pay off your mortgage faster by making the same or slightly higher payments to reduce your overall debt burden, and increase your long-term financial stability.

But here's the thing. Banks typically won't offer you lower rates, unless you ask, so it's essential to be proactive here. The bank pays around a thousand dollars in marketing costs to replace you, more if you used a mortgage broker, and that's your real negotiating power. To secure a rate reduction, research the rates offered by competitors, particularly online banks like ubank. And once you've gathered the lowest competitor's interest rate, prepare to negotiate with your current lender. I recommend that you also get in the habit of doing this for your loans and insurance policies once a year.

When speaking with your bank, be confident but polite. Explain that you've found lower rates elsewhere and are moving your loan, unless they can offer a competitive rate. Emphasize your value as a loyal customer, and your willingness to stay if they can match or improve upon the terms you found.

Call your bank, and ask for the customer retention team. When you're put through, follow this simple script:

> Hi, my name is ___***___, and I've been a loyal customer for [X years]. My account number is ___***___. I've applied to refinance my loan with [UBANK]. Their home loan interest rate is ___***___ percent, which is a full percent cheaper than you're charging me. Given our longstanding relationship, I would like you to match their offer, or send me the required forms to switch across to them."

The bank representative may ask you to hold while they review competitor rates and assess your repayment history. (Note: The goal here isn't actually to switch banks but to secure a better interest rate.) You're showing your willingness to move, which often prompts your bank to negotiate, as their retention team is highly motivated and has strict targets to meet. They're incentivized to offer discounts to profitable customers to retain them. The bank's response will probably be:

"We can't match that rate. However, as you're a valuable customer, we could offer you a zero point one five percent discount."

Your response should be:

"That's not good enough. I've already received conditional approval, so to stay I would need at least a zero point two five percent discount. Would you please refer this to your supervisor? I'm happy to wait."

Bank representative will need to consult with a higher-up when the amount is out of their authority limit. They will usually put you on hold, and then come back and say:

"Upon reviewing your case, we can offer you that zero point two five percent discount on your current rate.."

You can then say:

"Excellent! Please confirm this new rate via email to me at [your email], and confirm that it will be applied as of start of business tomorrow. Thank you."

Banks want to keep good customers, so don't be afraid to ask! Even a small reduction in your mortgage rate can save you thousands over the life of the loan.

Using Balance Transfers and Debt Consolidation

Balance transfers can be a useful tool, but only if you can afford to pay off the balance in full before the interest-free period ends. If you're not confident your budget can handle it, stick to your current debt plan, and focus on regularly chipping away at your balances.

CHAPTER 7

Securing Your Future: Jakes story

When Jake was nineteen, he came to me for help. As he was just starting his career in the Australian Defence Force (ADF), he mentioned that he wanted to get into home ownership as quickly as possible.

From the start, I was impressed by his maturity. It wasn't every day you hear a young man in his late teens talk about securing his future in such a thoughtful way. So, I shared some lessons I'd learned over the years about budgeting, saving, and making smart investment choices.

Jake, determined as always, took the advice to heart and began coming up with his own strategies. He chose to live on base instead of moving in with his mates. That saved him a good chunk of money he would've otherwise spent on rent or living expenses. Instead of buying takeaway or eating out with his friends, he took to batch cooking meals, making big portions of healthy food to last the week. It wasn't glamorous, but it kept him focused on his goal. Even when he could've splurged on a newer car, Jake stuck with his old car that he called "just functional" and refused to upgrade, knowing that every dollar he saved brought him one step closer to his home ownership dream.

But he didn't stop there. Jake set up separate accounts for his savings goals, keeping his finances organized, and his long-term objective at the forefront of his mind. Each paycheck went directly into these accounts, so he never lost sight of his goal. By the time Jake was twenty-one, he was able to buy his first property. It wasn't flashy or fancy. It was a modest home, but it was his.

That first purchase in Cardiff, NSW was one of the best decisions he could've made. In less than eight years, the property more than doubled in value. His discipline and focus on saving and investing early paid off in a big way. Home ownership is a compulsory savings plan, forcing you to build equity while also adding significant value to your financial future.

Jake's path wasn't the quickest or easiest, but it was certainly one of the smartest. He not only created a solid foundation for his financial future but learned the value of setting and achieving long-term goals.

RULE 3
BORROW WISELY

Avoid Borrowing for Lifestyle Upgrades

It's tempting to taking on lifestyle debt like financing cars, furniture, or holidays. However, borrowing for things that don't generate income only creates more financial pressure. A healthy rule of thumb is to only borrow for investments or opportunities that grow your wealth, such as real estate, education, or business ventures.

Plan Before You Borrow

Before taking on any loan, plan with intent and consideration. For example, if you're deciding between a standard car model and a top-of-the-line version that costs $15,000 more, ask yourself these questions:

- What could that $15,000 do if I invested it instead?
- Will the extra features add long-term value or simply satisfy a short-term desire?
- What is the purpose or intent of this purchase?

These questions are relevant not only for cars but for any investment you make, including real estate. When taking out any loan, negotiate the terms and interest rate. Even small changes can significantly impact the total cost of your loan over time.

The time to get the best interest rate is when you create the initial loan. This is when the bank wants you most and will fight hardest to get you. But the interest rate isn't the only, or even main, consideration.

CHAPTER 7

The terms of the loan can have a much greater impact. You want the most basic loan you can get, as the ones with loads of bells and whistles, called extra features, usually cost you much more. And I promise you that most customers don't use them.

Avoid repayment holidays, fixing a portion of the loan, or anything else the bank suggests. What you want is the money to buy the home and the ability to repay the loan quicker and without penalty.

For example, did you know that the banks will often charge you a penalty if you pay out your loan early? Crazy, right? But it's true. Let's think about it for a moment. What is the bank's primary goal? To make lots of money and generate profit for their shareholders. They're in the business of making money, and they do that by charging interest and having lots of fees.

Here are some common examples of fees, now often called "prepayment penalties," because our government banned the term "exit fees." Look out for the following;

> Flat fee penalty

   The bank charges a predetermined flat fee if you pay off the loan early, regardless of how much time is left on the loan term.

> Percentage of remaining balance

   Some banks may charge a penalty based on a percentage of the remaining loan balance. For example, you might owe two–five percent of the remaining principle if you pay off the loan early.

> Interest penalty

   Certain loans may have a clause requiring you to pay the interest you would have paid over a specific period, such as the next few months, even if you repay the loan in full.

> "Rule of 78" penalty

   This method is used to front-load interest payments during the early months of a loan. If you pay off your loan early, you may still be responsible for a significant portion of the interest, effectively reducing the financial benefit of early repayment.

- Breakage fees

    In some cases, such as fixed-rate mortgages, banks may charge a "breakage fee" to compensate for the lender's loss of interest income due to early repayment.

- Early termination fee

    This type of fee may be specified in the loan agreement and is simply a charge for ending the loan term early, regardless of the interest rate implications.

So for us savvy borrowers who want to pay off the loans early, understanding the terms and knowing exactly what you're signing up for are critical to creating your financial success. And always remember to ask the bank manager or broker how you can pay it out early.

Celebrate Debt Milestones

Paying off debt is a huge achievement, so remember to celebrate your progress! Whether it's making the final payment on a credit card or paying off your car loan, acknowledge your hard work.

Set Meaningful Financial Goals for the Future

Managing debt effectively puts you in control, but it's only the beginning. You're now free to focus on meaningful financial goals that guide your next steps. In the next chapter, we'll explore how to set clear goals that align with your values and help you build a life of financial freedom. Let's set goals that inspire you and create a future you'll love.

CHAPTER 7

WEEK 7
SMALL STEPS TO THE FUTURE ABUNDANT YOU

- Identify and prioritize your debts.

    1. Make a list of all your debts, including balances, interest rates, and minimum payments.

    2. Decide whether to follow the snowball or avalanche method, based on your financial goals and motivation.

- Negotiate lower interest rates on your mortgage or loans.

    1. Compare competitor bank rates

    2. Call your lender, and ask for a lower interest rate on your mortgage or personal loans, using your competitor's rates as leverage.

- Pay off your credit cards as soon as possible, and destroy the card to avoid temptation.

- Focus on building savings instead of relying on credit for emergencies.

CHAPTER

COMPOUND INTEREST
Let Your Money Grow While You Sleep

If you start investing a hundred dollars a month at age twenty-five, you could retire with over one-million dollars. The secret? Time and consistency.

Investing isn't about luck but starting early and being consistent. The simplest and safest way to create your fortune is the magic ingredient that turns small investments into substantial wealth: compound interest. It's the force that allows your money to grow exponentially over time, earning interest on interest. The earlier you start, the more time you give your money to work for you, even while you sleep. Let's explore how you can harness the power of achieving long-term security.

CHAPTER 8

SECTION 1

THE POWER OF COMPOUND INTEREST

Compound interest is simple, yet powerful. When your savings or investments earn interest, and that interest earns additional interest, your wealth grows exponentially over time. This process accelerates the longer your money stays invested.

Imagine that you work really hard, managing to save and invest five-thousand dollars each year into a basic shares portfolio. For ten years, you reinvest your money and its dividends in high-interest-earning stocks, achieving an average annual return of ten percent. After this ten-year period, you stop adding new money.

Meanwhile, your friend delays starting until age twenty-five, when they have a stable job. Unlike you, they continue contributing five thousand every year, until they turn sixty, ultimately investing a total of $180,000, compared to your $50,000.

So you'd expect them to have more money than you, right? Surprisingly, it's not the case. Despite contributing less than a third of what they invested, you end up with fifty percent more. Yours grows to $2,709,677 while theirs reaches $1,645,197. And that, my friend, is the power of compound interest at work.

This isn't a new concept, nor is it a matter of chance. It consistently works, every single time! It remains one of the safest and most reliable ways to build substantial wealth. So why doesn't everyone just do this? Simple. It's boring. But it's also effective. Let me show you.

COMPOUND INTEREST

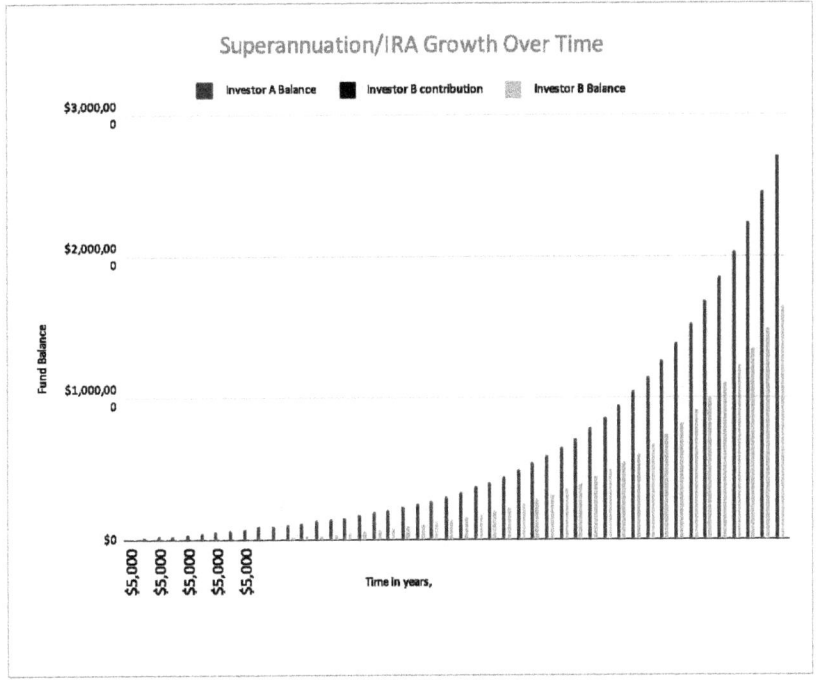

CHAPTER 8

Age	Investor A Contribution	Investor A Balance	Investor B contribution	Investor B Balance
15	$5,000	$ 5,500	$	$ -
16	$5,000	$ 11,550	$	$ -
17	$5,000	$ 18,205	$	$ -
18	$5,000	$ 25,526	$	$ -
19	$5,000	$ 33,578	$	$ -
20	$5,000	$ 42,436	$	$ -
21	$5,000	$ 52,179	$	$ -
22	$5,000	$ 62,897	$	$ -
23	$5,000	$ 74,687	$	$ -
24	$5,000	$ 87,656	$	$ -
25		$ 96,421	$5,000	$ 5,500
26		$ 106,064	$5,000	$ 11,550
27		$ 116,670	$5,000	$ 18,205
28		$ 128,337	$5,000	$ 25,526
29		$ 141,171	$5,000	$ 33,578
30		$ 155,288	$5,000	$ 42,436
31		$ 170,816	$5,000	$ 52,179
32		$ 187,898	$5,000	$ 62,897
33		$ 206,688	$5,000	$ 74,687
34		$ 227,357	$5,000	$ 87,656
35		$ 250,092	$5,000	$ 101,921
36		$ 275,102	$5,000	$ 117,614
37		$ 302,612	$5,000	$ 134,875
38		$ 332,873	$5,000	$ 153,862
39		$ 366,160	$5,000	$ 174,749
40		$ 402,776	$5,000	$ 197,724
41		$ 443,054	$5,000	$ 222,996
42		$ 487,359	$5,000	$ 250,795
43		$ 536,095	$5,000	$ 281,375
44		$ 589,705	$5,000	$ 315,012
45		$ 648,675	$5,000	$ 352,014
46		$ 713,543	$5,000	$ 392,715
47		$ 784,897	$5,000	$ 437,487
48		$ 863,387	$5,000	$ 486,735
49		$ 949,725	$5,000	$ 540,909
50		$ 1,044,698	$5,000	$ 600,500
51		$ 1,149,167	$5,000	$ 666,050
52		$ 1,264,084	$5,000	$ 738,155
53		$ 1,390,493	$5,000	$ 817,470
54		$ 1,529,542	$5,000	$ 904,717
55		$ 1,682,496	$5,000	$ 1,000,689
56		$ 1,850,746	$5,000	$ 1,106,258
57		$ 2,035,820	$5,000	$ 1,222,383
58		$ 2,239,402	$5,000	$ 1,350,122
59		$ 2,463,343	$5,000	$ 1,490,634
60		$ 2,709,677	$5,000	$ 1,645,197

These figures include both capital gains and dividends, providing a comprehensive view of the market's performance during this period.

And I note, over the past forty years, the S&P 500 index, which represents a broad spectrum of US stocks, has achieved an average annual return of approximately 10.7 percent. In Australia, over the past forty years, the returns are slightly lower at 9.8 percent. So I've used ten percent as an easy calculation to demonstrate how important *time* is.

The Difference Between Saving and Investing

Saving is important, but it only preserves your wealth, it doesn't grow it. A savings account offers stability but minimal returns. Investing, on the other hand, allows you to grow your wealth over time by taking advantage of higher returns through the stock market, real estate, or other assets.

Case Study: Starting Early vs. Late

Let's look at two investors: Sarah and Tom. Sarah starts investing $100 a month at age twenty-five, while Tom waits until age forty to begin. Both earn an average annual return of seven percent, and they each stop investing at age sixty-five. Here's how much they accumulate:

Investor	Monthly Investment	Age Started	Age Stopped	Total Invested	Final Amount
Sarah	$100	25	65	$48,000	$244,692
Tom	$100	40	65	$30,000	$76,120

Because Sarah started fifteen years earlier, her investment grows almost three times larger than Tom's, despite only investing $18,000 more. Time matters when it comes to investing!

CHAPTER 8

SECTION 2
INVESTMENT OPTIONS EXPLAINED

Stocks

When you buy stocks in a company, in Australia we call them shares, you essentially become a partial owner, with your ownership proportionate to the number of shares you hold. Companies issue stocks to raise capital for growth and expansion, and in return, investors get the opportunity to benefit from the company's success through price appreciation and dividends. Stockholders can also receive voting rights, giving them a say in major company decisions, depending on the type of stock they own.

> Benefits

1. Stocks have the potential for high returns, making them a key component of many investment portfolios.

2. Over the long term, they often outperform other types of investments, such as bonds and savings accounts.

3. They also offer dividend income that provides a steady cash flow to investors.

4. Investing in stocks allows for portfolio diversification across different sectors and industries, which can help mitigate risk.

5. As stocks are highly liquid, they can be easily bought and sold on exchanges, giving investors flexibility and access to their funds when needed.

Bonds

Bonds are debt securities issued by governments, municipalities, or corporations to raise capital. When you buy a bond, you're essentially lending money to the issuer in exchange for regular interest payments over a specified period, followed by the repayment of the bond's principal amount upon maturity. Bonds are generally considered a safer investment compared to stocks, as they offer predictable income through fixed interest payments, also known as coupons.

> Benefits

1. Bonds provide a stable and predictable income stream, making them an attractive option for conservative investors or those seeking steady cash flow, especially in retirement.

2. They're less volatile than stocks, so there's a level of portfolio stability, particularly during market downturns.

3. Bonds can act as a diversification tool that reduces overall investment risk when included in a mixed-asset portfolio.

4. Certain ones, such as government bonds, are considered low-risk, which means it's a safe place to preserve capital.

5. They also offer potential tax advantages. For instance, municipal bonds offer tax-exempt interest.

Retirement Accounts

Retirement accounts are financial accounts specifically designed to help individuals save and invest for their retirement years. Common examples include 401(k)s and IRAs in the United States, or superannuation in Australia. These accounts offer advantages, such as tax-deferred growth on investments or tax deductions for contributions to retirement accounts that can be made by individuals, employers, or both, depending on the type of account. And funds typically remain invested, until the account holder reaches retirement age.

➢ Benefits

1. The primary benefit of retirement accounts is their ability to grow investments tax-free or tax-deferred, so there's compound growth over time.

2. By delaying taxes on earnings, they maximize the potential for wealth accumulation, and many offer employer contributions or matching programs, which immediately boosts your savings.

3. Retirement accounts include a wide range of investment options, such as stocks, bonds, and mutual funds, which means portfolio diversification is tailored to your risk tolerance and retirement goals.

4. Built-in incentives for long-term saving provide a structured, disciplined approach as you go into retirement.

Managed Investments

Managed investments involve pooling money from multiple investors, which is then overseen by professional fund managers who make investment decisions on behalf of the investors. They select and manage a diversified portfolio of assets, such as stocks, bonds, real estate, or other securities. Examples of managed investments include mutual funds, hedge funds, and managed accounts. This approach allows individual investors to access professionally curated investment strategies and expertise without having to manage their investments on a daily basis.

➢ Benefits

1. The primary benefit of managed investments is the expertise and professional oversight provided by experienced fund managers, which leads to better-informed investment decisions, potentially increasing returns while minimizing risks through diversification.

2. Managed funds are ideal for individuals who prefer a hands-off approach, as the day-to-day research, asset allocation, and market monitoring are handled by professionals.

3. These funds offer access to a broad range of asset classes and markets that might be challenging or impractical for individual investors to manage on their own. This diversification can strengthen portfolio stability and reduce risk.

Listed Investment Companies (LICs)

Listed investment companies (LICs) are pooled investment funds that trade on a stock exchange, much like regular stocks. Unlike exchange-traded funds (ETFs), LICs are actively managed by a professional team that makes decisions about which assets to buy and sell within the portfolio. They typically have a closed-ended structure, meaning they raise a fixed amount of capital through an initial public offering (IPO), and then list it on the exchange. As a result, the number of shares in circulation remains constant, which can offer stability and reduce market volatility compared to open-ended funds.

- Benefits
    1. One key benefit of LICs is professional management, where experienced fund managers actively select and manage investments to achieve specific performance goals. This can offer potential for superior returns compared to passive index-tracking investments.
    2. They provide diversification across different asset classes, sectors, or markets, which reduces risk.
    3. Since LICs are traded on the stock exchange, they're relatively easy to buy and sell.
    4. The closed-ended structure of LICs prevents the need for constant inflows and outflows of funds, so managers can focus on long-term strategies without being forced to sell assets to meet redemptions.
    5. They're a convenient option if you want a blend of active management and stability in your investment portfolio.

CHAPTER 8

Exchange-Traded Funds (ETFs)

Exchange-traded funds (ETFs) are investment funds that are traded on stock exchanges, much like individual stocks. They typically aim to track the performance of a specific index, sector, commodity, or asset class by holding a diversified portfolio that mirrors the index or category they're designed to replicate. Unlike mutual funds, which can only be traded at the end of the trading day, ETFs are bought and sold throughout the day, offering real-time pricing. This makes ETFs flexible and accessible for both novice and experienced investors.

➤ Benefits

1. By investing in an ETF, you gain exposure to a broad range of assets, reducing individual security risk.

2. They tend to have lower fees than actively managed funds, due to their passive management approach, which helps grow long-term returns.

3. ETFs offer liquidity, as they can be traded throughout the day at market prices, making it easier for investors to enter or exit positions quickly.

4. They're highly transparent, with holdings regularly disclosed, so it provides clarity on the exact assets you own.

Direct Investments

Direct investments refer to purchasing individual assets, such as stocks, bonds, or real estate, without the involvement of an intermediary or pooled fund. By investing directly, you have full control over your investment choices, including which assets to buy, sell, or hold, and when to execute transactions. This approach allows for customized investment strategies tailored to specific goals, risk tolerance, and market outlook. Direct investments can be made through brokerage accounts or other platforms that facilitate asset purchases.

➢ Benefits

1. Unlike managed funds, where investment decisions are made by a manager, direct investors can craft a highly personalized portfolio and make timely decisions based on their financial goals.

2. This flexibility leads to cost savings, as fees associated with direct investments are typically lower than those for managed funds.

3. Direct investments provide transparency, so investors know exactly what assets they hold and how each is performing. This approach presents opportunities for targeted tax management, such as tax-loss harvesting, to optimize returns. For experienced investors, direct investments offer the potential for significant returns and active engagement in their financial journey.

Real Estate as a Wealth-Building Tool

Most real estate purchased as an investment won't necessarily generate significant income, which is why so many financial planners are hesitant to recommend it as a viable option. However, it's important to note that not all real estate investments are the same. Traditional investment properties are often negatively geared rental properties, so that means they actually cost you money to hold onto them while you get a tax break. To truly succeed, you need a strategic approach to real estate investing.

Focus on cash-flow-positive properties with multiple income streams, such as homes with granny flats, duplexes, rooming houses, or boarding houses. These types of properties offer consistent income while covering their expenses. Alternatively, subdivisions or small development projects can deliver substantial onetime profits, making them an attractive option for experienced investors.

If you're interested in maximizing real estate profits, be sure to explore my other book, *Property Power*, for an in-depth guide to successful real estate strategies.

CHAPTER 8

Conclusion

No matter where you choose to direct your money, I recommend selecting an option that aligns with your risk profile and personal needs, and then immersing yourself in learning about that area or paying the fees to have an expert do it for you.

I chose to become proficient in real estate investing. However, if you're like me when it comes to stocks and bonds, and feel a bit too unmotivated to learn every detail, or if you simply can't decide, consider choosing a habit that you can consistently maintain. A great example is putting any extra money into your superannuation, where the fund managers handle everything for you. Simple and effective!

Make sure you select the right mix of these investment vehicles, so you can build a robust and diversified portfolio tailored to your financial goals and risk tolerance.

SECTION 3

CREATING A HABIT OF INVESTING: MAKE IT PART OF YOUR ROUTINE

- Automate Your Investments Monthly

    The easiest way to invest consistently is to automate your contributions. Set up automatic transfers from your bank account into your chosen investment fund or account each month. This eliminates decision fatigue, and your investments stay on track no matter what life throws your way.

- Invest During Market Downturns

    It's completely natural to feel anxious during market downturns, but these moments can actually present valuable buying opportunities. By maintaining your investments through both favorable and challenging market conditions, you harness the power of dollar-cost averaging. This strategy involves purchasing more shares when prices are low, and fewer when prices are high, to reduce your average cost per share over time.

    The benefits of this approach are numerous. First, it helps take the emotion out of investing, because it's consistent, not reactionary. Second, it positions you to capture gains when the market eventually rebounds, so you maximize potential returns on the shares acquired at lower prices. Finally, dollar-cost averaging supports a disciplined, long-term investment mindset, which is a key habit to building wealth steadily and weathering market volatility with confidence.

CHAPTER 8

> Review and Rebalance Yearly

Set aside time each year to thoroughly review your portfolio, and assess whether your investments align with your current financial goals, risk tolerance, and market conditions. Over time, certain investments may grow faster than others, where it shifts away from your intended strategy. This can expose you to risks that may not suit your long-term objectives or reduce the diversification you once had.

Rebalancing involves making adjustments to restore the original target allocation of your investments. For example, if one asset class, such as stocks, has grown significantly and now represents a larger portion of your portfolio than intended, you might sell some of those holdings. Then redistribute the funds into underperforming or less-represented areas, such as bonds or other assets to manage risk and guarantee your portfolio stays aligned with your desired balance between growth and stability.

Rebalancing offers an opportunity to take profits from well-performing investments and potentially buy undervalued assets, which supports the "buy low, sell high" strategy.

My Grandmother's Missed Opportunity: A Story

My grandmother bought a lotto ticket every week, dreaming of striking it rich. She spent decades chasing luck but never winning big. If she'd instead invested that twenty dollars per week, she would have retired with over $500,000 in a simple stock portfolio. The lesson? Invest regularly, even with small amounts, and let compound interest do the work.

To look at it another way, if she'd invested that same money in a simple stock portfolio, she would have accumulated over $4,161,154, which is twenty dollars per week for sixty years, compounding at ten percent, all thanks to the power of compound interest. The money she spent on lottery tickets, which never paid off, could have worked for her, steadily growing year after year.

The lesson from my grandmother's experience is clear: wealth isn't about luck or waiting for a windfall. It's about consistency and patience over time. Small, regular investments, even modest ones, can grow into substantial wealth when given enough time to compound.

The real key to financial success doesn't lie in hoping for an instant payout, but in making wise choices and sticking with them. Compound interest, turns small amounts into something much larger. My grandmother's story taught me that the true power of wealth lies in regular investment, and the steady accumulation of value.

Protect Your Wealth

Investing is a great way to build wealth, but it's only one part of the equation. To truly secure your financial future, you must plan for your success. In the next chapter, we'll dive into strategies to keep you moving toward financial freedom.

CHAPTER 8

WEEK 8
SMALL STEPS TO THE FUTURE ABUNDANT YOU

- Choose your investment path.
  - ✓ Reflect on your personal goals and risk tolerance to determine which type of investment suits you best. Are you looking for steady, low-risk options like bonds, or are you comfortable with the potential ups and downs of shares or long term growth of real estate?
  - Make a decision based on both your short-term goals, like saving for a home, and long-term goals, like building wealth for retirement.

- Automate your monthly investments.
  - ✓ Set up an automatic transfer from your high-interest savings account into your chosen investment vehicle, whether it's shares, bonds, ETFs, or managed funds. Stay consistent, no matter how busy life gets. Let compound growth work for you.

CHAPTER

EVALUATE FINANCIAL GOALS

Without goals, money slips away.
But when you give it a mission, it works wonders.

Clear financial goals align your money with your values. They give focus to your financial decisions and keep you motivated through challenges. Let's explore how to set purposeful goals, break them down into achievable steps, and stay on track, even when life throws you a curveball.

CHAPTER 9

SECTION 1
ALIGN GOALS WITH VALUES

Money becomes truly powerful when it supports what matters most to you. By identifying your core values, such as family, adventure, security, freedom, or any personal priorities, you give yourself direction and purpose. Aligning your financial goals with these values leads to a meaningful, fulfilling life.

To start, reflect on what you genuinely care about, and what brings you happiness and fulfillment. What do you want your legacy to be? What brings you the most joy? Once you clarify these values, use them as a compass to set clear, intentional financial goals.

For example:

- Family-focused goal:
    - ✓ Create an education fund for children.
    - ✓ Build a comfortable family home
    - ✓ Fund family experiences that create lasting memories.
- Adventure-focused goal:
    - ✓ Set up a dedicated savings plan for a year of travel, exploring new places, cultures, and experiences.
    - ✓ Invest in a travel fund
    - ✓ Create passive income streams to support an exploration lifestyle.
- Security-focused goal:
    - ✓ Prioritize building an emergency fund to cover unexpected expenses, followed by a solid retirement savings plan to guarantee long-term financial stability.

✓ Pay down debt, or invest in assets that offer consistent returns.

➤ Freedom-focused goal

✓ Work toward financial independence to start a business or have flexibility.

✓ Create passive income streams to cover all retirement expenses.

When your financial goals are driven by your values, each dollar you save or invest becomes a step toward living the life you truly want. You'll have a deeper sense of satisfaction, as you see your money helping you fulfill what matters most.

Long-Term vs. Short-Term Goals

Balancing short-term goals with long-term objectives is essential for being fulfilled and secure. Short-term goals allow you to enjoy and experience life in the present. They offer a sense of reward and satisfaction, as they often come to fruition relatively quickly, which reinforces positive money habits and gives you the motivation to continue saving and planning.

Long-term goals provide stability and security. They may take years to achieve, but they lay the foundation, and you'll be prepared for life's unexpected challenges.

To strike the right balance, it's important to prioritize and allocate resources wisely. This might mean creating a budget that divides your savings into different buckets for immediate and future needs or setting up automatic transfers. This assures you won't be sacrificing your long-term dreams and security, and you get to experience the best of both worlds of living fully in the present while building a solid foundation for the future.

The 60/20/10/10 DEAL budget strategy works here as well.

CHAPTER 9

Case Study: Creating a Life of Luxury

Back in the 1990s, when I first met Len, he had no real concept of banking or finances. He was using an old-fashioned passport-style savings account that earned almost no interest, and he didn't know how to manage money or plan for his financial future. It became immediately clear to me that he was missing some crucial financial knowledge that could truly benefit him. So, as his partner at the time, I decided to take matters into my own hands, and show him the ropes.

The first step I took was changing his savings account to one with a much higher interest rate. I showed him how to use an ATM for the first time, explaining how to check balances, make deposits, and withdraw cash. It was a simple change, but for Len, it was like opening the door to a whole new world of financial possibilities.

Next, I encouraged him to sit down with a financial planner, someone who could help him navigate the more complicated aspects of his investing. Together, they set up a share portfolio and superannuation account, and I helped him automate his pay so that every payday, a portion of his income was funneled directly into the correct accounts. I explained how, over time, the money would grow with compound interest, and how this would become an essential source of income when it came time to retire.

Over the next few decades, Len became more involved in his finances. With each pay cycle, he continued his contributions, which steadily grew, and as the years passed, his investments compounded. Len didn't just save. He was intentional about where he placed his money, and his overtime and bonuses were working hard in higher-yielding investments. By the time Len stopped working, his savings had compounded for over thirty years. He had more than enough to support a lifestyle of luxury, enjoying the fruits of his diligent saving and smart investment decisions.

With the financial security he built, Len enjoys a luxurious retirement, free from the worries that plague so many who neglect their financial futures. His superannuation, the smart decisions we made together, and the power of compound interest, have provided a calm and peaceful life, and I'm proud that I helped him get there.

SECTION 2
SMARTIE FINANCIAL GOALS

The SMARTIE framework helps you create goals that are actionable, meaningful, and aligned with your values. Here's how it works:

- **S**pecific

    Be clear about what you want to achieve, such as, "pay off my $5,000 credit card balance."

- **M**easurable

    Define how you'll track your progress. For instance, if you're saving for a vacation, and you've set up a separate account, you can clearly see how close you are to your target.

- **A**chievable

    Your goal should be realistic based on your current income and expenses.

- **R**elevant

    Make sure it aligns with your values and long-term vision.

- **T**ime-bound

    Set a deadline, like having the full amount of your credit card debt paid off by a certain date.

- **I**ntuitive

    The goal should feel right to you. Listen to your gut instincts.

CHAPTER 9

> ➤ Emotional
>
> Tie your goal to a personal desire and how it will feel to keep you motivated, like knowing you're in control and being able to let go of money worries.

Break Large Goals into Milestones

Big goals can feel overwhelming, but breaking them down into smaller milestones makes them more manageable. For example, if your goal is to save $50,000 for a home deposit, start with a milestone of $5,000. Celebrate when you reach each one to maintain momentum.

Use Visual Tools

Visual goal trackers, like charts, apps, or even a physical savings jar, help you see your progress. Watching your savings grow or your debt shrink, reinforces positive habits and keeps you motivated.

SECTION 3

TRACKING AND ADJUSTING GOALS

Make it a habit to review your financial progress. Assess where you are with each goal, and adjust if necessary. If you're on track, celebrate your wins. Each milestone achieved deserves recognition.

Review Progress

Time-based cues are specific moments or intervals that trigger an action to keep you on track with your goals. Here are some examples:

> Morning Routine

  Set aside time each morning, like ten minutes right after waking up, to review your daily or weekly goals.

> Weekly Review

  Every Sunday evening, spend fifteen-twenty minutes reflecting on your progress for the week and planning the upcoming week's goals.

> Monthly Check-In

  At the start of each month, set a reminder to review your broader goals, assess whether you're on track, and make necessary adjustments to stay aligned.

> Quarterly Reflection

  Every three months, schedule a deeper dive into your goals to evaluate your progress, and reassess your strategies. This can include a thorough review of both successes and areas needing improvement.

CHAPTER 9

- Daily Time Blocks

    Set specific times in your calendar for focused work on particular tasks.

- End-of-Day Review

    Set a cue at the end of each workday to briefly evaluate what you accomplished, check if your tasks were aligned with your goals, and prepare for the next day.

These time-based cue tasks create structure in your day, so your goals stay front and center, while making it easier to take consistent action.

Set up a schedule that will work for you. The more frequent your check-ins, the easier it is to adjust when needed. Make it a habit to review your financial progress. Assess where you are with each goal, and adjust if necessary. If you're on track, celebrate your wins. Each milestone achieved deserves recognition.

Adjusting Goals

Life is full of changes. New jobs or relationships, having children, and experiencing job loss. When these shifts occur, adjust your financial goals accordingly. It's okay to change direction as your life evolves, as long as your goals remain aligned with your values and long-term vision.

Daily Actions Drive Progress

Now that you have clear financial goals in place, it's time to take action. In the next chapter, we'll explore the daily habits and routines that will keep you on track, moving steadily toward your goals. Let's dive into the small, consistent actions that create big financial results.

EVALUATE FINANCIAL GOALS

WEEK 9
THE FUTURE ABUNDANT YOU

- Set your money goals.

    Identify and define your financial goals, from immediate priorities to long-term dreams. Make sure each goal is aligned with your personal values.

- Review your financial position.

    Commit to regular financial check-ins every month, quarter, and at the end of each year. This will help you track your progress, celebrate milestones, and make adjustments as needed.

- Adjust your goals.

    At every financial review, adjust and refine your goals for the next period. Life evolves, and so should your financial plan. It might mean tweaking your savings target, adding a new goal, or shifting priorities to reflect your current situation.

- Celebrate.

    Mark every small step that takes you toward the future abundant you.

CHAPTER

FINANCIAL FREEDOM IN RETIREMENT

Turning Your Money Power into a Secure Retirement

You've already started applying the *ABUNDANCE* steps, transforming your financial habits, eliminating debt, and building wealth. Now, it's time to take the next crucial step of making sure you're financially set for a lifetime.

Retirement isn't just about reaching a certain age but having the financial security to live on your terms. But do you know exactly how much you'll need? Will your current savings and investments sustain the lifestyle you envision?

CHAPTER 10

In this chapter, we'll apply the *ABUNDANCE* principles to assess your current financial position, determine your retirement target, and bridge any gaps between where you are now and where you want to be, so your future is just as abundant.

Why Planning Matters

Retirement is one of life's biggest financial milestones, yet many people approach it with uncertainty rather than clarity. Without a solid plan, financial stress can replace what should be a time of freedom and fulfillment. That's why assessing your current financial position and determining exactly what you'll need for retirement, is crucial.

Where you are vs. where you need to be

Many people assume they'll figure out their retirement finances as they go, but a vague approach can lead to unexpected shortfalls.

By assessing your savings, investments, income streams, and expenses, you gain a clear picture of your financial health. From there, you can define what a comfortable retirement looks like for you, and create a strategy to achieve it. The key is knowing exactly what you need to make it a reality.

Guessing vs. calculating

A common mistake people make is assuming they'll "need about a million dollars" or relying on vague rules of thumb without real calculations. But retirement planning isn't one-size-fits-all. Your financial needs depend on factors like your desired lifestyle, expected expenses, potential healthcare costs, and how long you'll need your money to last.

Instead of guessing, you need a personalized financial plan that considers

- your ideal monthly and annual retirement budget
- your projected income from savings, investments, and pensions
- inflation and how it impacts your future purchasing power

- potential healthcare costs and unforeseen expenses.

Crunch the numbers rather than making assumptions, and you'll make decisions based on facts, not hope.

Laying the foundation

When you have a clear retirement strategy, you remove the anxiety of wondering whether your money will last. A well-thought-out plan means you retire on your terms, without the fear of running out of money or having to make drastic lifestyle changes later in life.

Taking control of your financial future today means you're not just planning for retirement, you're giving yourself a lifetime of financial freedom.

In the next sections, we'll walk through the key steps to determine exactly how much you need to retire, assess your current position, and create a roadmap to close any gaps. Let's build your stress-free, financially secure retirement, starting now.

CHAPTER 10

SECTION 1
ASSESSING YOUR CURRENT FINANCIAL POSITION

Before you can create a solid retirement plan, you need to understand exactly where you stand financially. Just like a GPS needs a starting point before mapping out a route, your retirement begins with assessing your current assets, debts, income, and expenses. It provides a clear, realistic snapshot of your financial health and helps identify any gaps between where you are now and where you need to be.

Taking inventory of your financial assets

Your financial assets form the foundation of your retirement security. These include everything from savings accounts and investments, to real estate and income-generating assets. A detailed inventory lets you know how much wealth you've already built, and how these assets can support your retirement.

This involves evaluating your retirement accounts, such as 401(k)s, IRAs, or superannuation, the value of your home and other properties, and any passive income streams you may have. Knowing what you own and how much income it generates, will help you determine whether your assets are aligned with your long-term financial goals.

Answer the following questions to help gain clarity:

➤ What are your current savings and investments?

➤ Do you have any retirement accounts, such as a 401k, an IRA, or superannuation?

➤ What is the total value of your assets, like your home, stocks, or businesses?

➤ How much passive income, which includes dividends and rental income, do you currently have?

Understanding your debts and liabilities

Carrying high-interest debt or long-term liabilities can drain your savings, reduce your monthly cash flow, and increase financial stress. That's why it's essential to take stock of all your outstanding debts, including your mortgage, and other loans, or any other financial obligations. Understanding how much you owe and the timeline for repayment, will help you develop a strategy to reduce or eliminate them before retirement. The less debt you have, the more financial flexibility you'll enjoy in your golden years.

Questions that will help you gain clarity:

➤ What debts are outstanding? Tip: Look back at your financial snapshot from chapter three.

➤ How long will it take to pay them off?

➤ How much of your monthly budget is dedicated to debt repayment? It should be twenty percent of your income or more, if you're able.

Evaluating your current income and expenses

Retirement planning isn't just about saving but also managing your income and expenses effectively. Your current income, including employment, side businesses, or investments, plays a crucial role in how much you can set aside for the future.

Equally important is understanding your spending habits. Your fixed expenses, like rent and insurance, and variable expenses, like entertainment and travel, shows you where your money is going and how much you can allocate toward retirement savings.

Having an emergency fund in place means financial setbacks won't derail your plans.

CHAPTER 10

Questions that will help you gain clarity:

- What is your annual income. This includes your salary and any side incomes or investments.?
- What are your fixed and variable expenses?
- How much are you currently saving per month/year for retirement?
- Do you have a sufficient emergency fund in place?

SECTION 2
DETERMINING YOUR RETIREMENT NEEDS

Once you've assessed your current financial position, the next step is to determine how much money you'll need to retire comfortably. Retirement is about achieving financial freedom, so you can maintain your desired lifestyle without worrying about running out of money.

To do this, you need to estimate your future expenses, identify all possible income sources, and set a realistic savings target. By taking a strategic, numbers-driven approach, you can create a roadmap for financial security and ensure you have enough to enjoy your retirement years stress-free.

Estimating your future expenses

A successful retirement plan starts with understanding how much you'll need to cover your future expenses. Many people underestimate their retirement costs, assuming they will naturally spend less. However, expenses such as housing, food, utilities, transportation, and healthcare continue, and in some cases, even increase with age.

Your retirement lifestyle will impact how much money you need, so factoring in potential healthcare costs, inflation, and any dependents you may need to support, is crucial.

Questions that will help you gain clarity:

- How much will you need for basic living expenses?
- What lifestyle do you want in retirement? Modest, comfortable, or luxurious? (Consider travel, hobbies, entertainment, gifts, and philanthropy.)

CHAPTER 10

> How will healthcare costs factor into your budget?

> Will you have dependents or family responsibilities in retirement?

Identifying future income sources

To build a strong retirement plan, you need to know where your income will come from once you stop working full-time. While traditional pensions and government benefits can provide a foundation, they may not be enough to sustain your ideal lifestyle.

That's why it's important to evaluate additional income sources, such as rental properties, dividend-paying investments, annuities, or passive business income. Some retirees also choose to work part-time or start a side business to supplement their income.

Questions that will help you gain clarity:

> What pensions or government benefits will you be eligible for?

> Will you receive any rental or passive business income?

> Will you continue working part-time or start a side business?

Setting a retirement savings target

Now that you understand your projected expenses and income sources, it's time to determine exactly how much you need to save to retire comfortably. This involves calculating a savings target based on your expected annual withdrawals, and the longevity of your funds.

Many financial experts use the four percent rule, which suggests that withdrawing four percent of your retirement savings annually can help your money last for thirty years. However, factors such as investment returns, inflation, and personal risk tolerance must be considered.

Questions that will help you gain clarity:

> How much money will you need to retire comfortably?

- What is the projected return on your investments?
- How long do you expect your retirement funds to last?

CHAPTER 10

SECTION 3
THE RETIREMENT GAP

After assessing your current financial position and determining how much you'll need for retirement, the next step is identifying any gaps between the two. Many people assume they're on track for retirement, until they do the math and realize they may fall short. The retirement gap is the difference between your projected financial needs and your current savings, investments, and income sources.

Understanding this gap allows you to take proactive steps to close it before it becomes a problem. This section will help you compare your estimated retirement expenses to your existing savings, determine how much more you need to save, and factor the long-term aspect of inflation.

Comparing projected needs vs. current situation

Figuring out if your current financial resources will generate enough income to sustain your desired lifestyle requires an honest assessment of your savings, investments, pensions, and passive income sources versus your expected retirement expenses. If your projected income falls short of your anticipated needs, adjustments must be made to avoid financial strain in retirement.

➢ Identifying shortfalls

If a gap exists between what you have and what you'll need, it's essential to calculate exactly how much more you should be saving. Determine a target savings rate based on factors like your retirement timeline, expected investment returns, and projected withdrawal rate. The earlier you identify a shortfall, the more time you have to adjust your strategy, such as increasing savings, extending your working years, or optimizing your investments.

> Understanding the impact of inflation

One of the most overlooked factors in retirement planning is inflation. Over time, the cost of living rises, meaning that what seems like a comfortable retirement fund today may not be sufficient in the future. Inflation erodes purchasing power, making everyday expenses more costly as years go by.

Inflation eats away at purchasing power. The rule of 72 helps estimate how long it will take for your money to lose half its value due to inflation.

Formula 72 ÷ inflation rate = years to half

Example: if inflation is 4.5% per year:

72 ÷ 4.5 = 16 years

That means that in 16 years, your nest egg would buy only half as much as it does today if it isn't invested to grow.

So, if you don't invest your money and inflation is 4.5%, your $500,000 today would feel like $250,000 in 16 years.

This rule works for both positive growth, like investments, and negative effects like inflation eating away your purchasing power.

CHAPTER 10

SECTION 4
ACTION STEPS

Once you've identified a potential shortfall, it's time to take action. Here are several strategic steps you can take to close the retirement gap, and secure your financial future.

> Increasing contributions to retirement accounts and investments

One of the most effective ways to close the gap is increasing contributions to your retirement savings, like maximizing contributions to a 401(k), IRA, or superannuation. If you're behind on savings, consider taking advantage of catch-up contributions, which allow people over a certain age to contribute more. Investing wisely in diversified assets with a strong long-term growth potential can also accelerate wealth accumulation.

> Diversifying income streams

Relying solely on one source of income in retirement, such as Social Security or a pension, can be risky. Diversifying your income streams provides financial stability and helps protect against unexpected changes in the economy. Consider building additional sources of income through rental properties, dividend-paying stocks, or freelance consulting. Having multiple income sources means you have more financial flexibility and security.

> Reducing unnecessary expenses

Another effective way to bridge the retirement gap is reassessing your current spending habits and finding areas where you can cut back. It's easy to slip into old spending habits, so doing this will allow you to objectively review your situation.

Remember that this doesn't mean sacrificing your quality of life but rather making smarter financial choices. Reducing discretionary spending like luxury purchases can free up more money to be redirected into retirement savings. Downsizing your home or eliminating high-interest debt can also have a significant impact on long-term financial security.

➤ Seeking professional advice

Financial planning is complex, and working with a professional can help you make the best decisions for your future. A certified financial planner (CFP) or retirement specialist helps assess your specific situation, optimize your investment portfolio, and provide tailored strategies to maximize your savings and minimize tax liabilities. Professional guidance makes a significant difference in guaranteeing your retirement plan is both realistic and sustainable.

CHAPTER 10

SECTION 5
CREATING YOUR PERSONALIZED RETIREMENT PLAN

For your retirement plan, create a strategy that evolves with your life and financial situation. Set clear goals, monitor progress, and make adjustments as needed to stay on track.

- Setting clear savings and investment goals

  Establishing clear, achievable financial goals is the foundation of a successful retirement plan. Define how much you need to save each year, where you will invest those savings, and what return you expect on your investments. Your goals should be specific and measurable, based on your income and retirement timeline. Remember to be a SMARTIE with your goals!

- Tracking progress and adjusting

  Retirement planning isn't a one-time event - it requires ongoing monitoring and adjustments. Regularly reviewing your financial position helps you stay on track to meet your goals. Market fluctuations, changes in income, or unexpected expenses may require modifications to your savings strategy. Make proactive changes rather than reacting to financial challenges later in life.

- Developing a timeline

  Knowing when you can retire comfortably is just as important as being aware of how much you need. Your retirement timeline should align with your financial readiness and personal goals. You may choose to retire early or work longer to maximize savings and benefits.

Creating a timeline helps you establish key milestones, such as when to reduce work hours, when to start withdrawing from retirement accounts, or transition fully into retirement.

Final thoughts

Financial freedom in retirement begins with careful planning, informed decision-making, and taking consistent action steps.

CONCLUSION
Money Habits for Life

Summary

Mastering your money habits isn't something you achieve overnight. It takes time, patience, and practice, but each step builds on the last, creating a solid foundation. It works, because one habit naturally leads to the next, and in the end, you'll live a life of financial ABUNDANCE.

CONCLUSION

- **A**wareness

    You now have a clear understanding of how your money flows, along with the habits, beliefs, and emotions that unlock the power to change.

- **B**alance

    You've aligned your spending with your values, creating a lifestyle where you enjoy today while securing your future. You no longer feel torn between living in the moment and planning for tomorrow.

- **U**nderstanding

    You have full clarity on where your money goes, so you make smarter decisions about spending, saving, and investing. No more confusion. Just control and confidence in your financial choices.

- **N**otice

    You've developed the habit of checking in regularly with your budget and making adjustments when needed. When you're off track, you course-correct with ease.

- **D**isasters

    With your emergency fund securely in place, you're prepared for life's unexpected moments. What once would have caused financial stress is now just a manageable hiccup.

- **A**llocate

    Through automation, you've taken the guesswork out of managing your money. Savings, investments, and bills are handled effortlessly without relying on willpower.

- **N**avigate

    You've paid off debt strategically and now borrow only for growth opportunities. Debt is no longer a burden, but a tool you use wisely when needed.

CONCLUSION

- **C**ompound

    You invest early, and stay consistent, letting your wealth grow steadily over time.

- **E**valuate

    You celebrate your milestones, review your progress, and adjust your goals to reflect your evolving life. With each step, you gain momentum, ensuring your journey stays aligned with what matters most.

Whether you're just starting out or starting over, applying these nine ABUNDANCE habits will guide you toward your own definition of financial freedom. They provide the structure and mindset needed to help you regain control, and align your money with your life goals and values. With consistent progress, you'll not only build financial security, but also create space for the things that matter most. Wherever you are, you'll have a reliable roadmap that empowers you.

The goal isn't perfection but consistent progress. Every small improvement adds up, creating a life where your money serves your goals, reduces anxiety, and builds lasting wealth.

CONCLUSION

YOUR JOURNEY STARTS NOW

TAKE THE FIRST STEP TODAY

Every great journey begins with a single step. You might want to become aware of your spending habits, track your expenses for the first time, or set a new financial goal. What matters most is starting. Financial mastery leads to long-term security.

Additional Support to Stay on Track Commitment Actions to the Future Wealthy You

You don't have to do this alone. If you're ready to take it to the next level, join our online coaching program. It will give you the support, tools, and accountability you need to stay on track, and reach your financial goals with confidence.

Your path toward ABUNDANCE begins now. Every small step matters. Let's walk it together.

www.ingramcontent.com/pod-product-compliance
Lightning Source LLC
Chambersburg PA
CBHW070801100426
42742CB00012B/2214